Inspirational Baseball Legends Stories, Facts and Trivia for Heroic Boys!

Harris Baker

Before we dive in, feel free to subscribe for free giveaways and all new book alerts!

Just scan the QR code below and stay connected with our community ;)

Contents

The Legendary Journeys of Baseball Heroes

Babe Ruth

The Sultan of Swat

Alright, folks, we are in a time long, long ago—like when dinosaurs roamed the Earth, but replace dinosaurs with horses and carriages, and swap out the cavemen for folks in bowler hats and suspenders. We're talking about the late 1800s, a world without TikTok or even television! This was the world George Herman Ruth Jr., who'd later become the legendary Babe Ruth, was born into on February 6, 1895, in Baltimore, Maryland—a city whose glory days were filled with harbors and heavenly crab cakes rather than baseball.

Little George, as they called him before he became the Sultan of Swat, didn't start out with an easy life. His family lived in a small, cramped apartment above the saloon his father owned—a place where grown-ups were constantly laughing loudly and singing off-key to old-timey tunes. Little George didn't mind it too much, though. He was more interested in running around the streets, getting into all sorts of trouble. Let's just say young George had a talent for chaos. He once said he was never taught any rules when he was a kid, and he seemed to prove it by breaking all of them!

School and George Ruth were like oil and water—they didn't mix. If there was a teacher's pet, George was the class clown's best friend. In fact, he was a bit of a wild child. By the time he was seven, his parents decided they definitely couldn't handle his rambunctious nature and sent him off to St. Mary's Industrial School for Boys. This wasn't your average school with recess and lunchboxes. St. Mary's was more like a military academy with a dash of strictness and a sprinkle of discipline. It was run by the Xaverian Brothers, who were really good at making boys behave well.

At St. Mary's, George met Brother Matthias, a towering figure who would later have a pivotal influence in his life. Brother Matthias was a big dude—like a human oak tree—and he had a talent for baseball. He recognized that George had a knack for the game—maybe because George could hit a baseball farther than anyone else at the school, or maybe because George was a natural pitcher who could throw a curveball that seemed to defy the laws of physics. Either way, Brother Matthias took George under his wing, teaching him baseball but also the importance of discipline and hard work.

While at St. Mary's, George spent countless hours on the baseball field. He played every position but shined brightest as a pitcher. Young George, barely a teenager, was hurling fastballs with such speed and accuracy that even the older boys would stand back in awe. It was at St. Mary's that George Herman Ruth Jr. began to transform into the baseball phenomenon we know as Babe Ruth. Here's a kid who started out as a bit of a rascal, with more energy than a room full of puppies, who found his passion in a place where most boys might have crumbled under the strict regime. Instead, George thrived, thanks to baseball and the mentorship of Brother Matthias.

The thing about George was that he had this larger-than-life personality, even as a kid. He was known for his hearty laugh, his mischievous grin, and his endless appetite. Seriously, this guy could eat more hot dogs than you can count. But more importantly, he had a heart as big as his appetite. He was the kind of kid who, despite his mischievous ways, would share his candy with the other boys and help out whenever he could.

By the time he turned 19, George's talents had caught the attention of Jack Dunn, the owner of the Baltimore Orioles—a minor league team, not to be confused with the major league team we know today. Dunn was so impressed with George's skills that he signed him to his first professional contract in 1914. And just like that, George Herman Ruth Jr. was catapulted into the world of professional baseball. The other players on the Orioles, seeing this young kid with a baby face, started calling him "Jack's newest babe." The nickname stuck, and soon, everyone was calling him Babe Ruth. Funny how things work out, huh?

But let's not jump ahead too quickly! Before Babe Ruth became the Colossus of Clout, the Sultan of Swat, or the Great Bambino, he was simply a young man with a dream, a powerful arm, and a bat that could send baseballs soaring into the stratosphere. It was these early years—full of mischief, discipline, and discovery—that laid the foundation for the legend he would become.

So there we were, with young George transformed into Babe Ruth, thanks to a nickname that stuck faster than bubble gum under a school desk. Babe was now part of the Baltimore Orioles, but don't let the minor league status fool you—this was a major step up from St. Mary's. Picture this: an excited, slightly bewildered 19-year-old stepping into the world of professional baseball with dreams as big as his swing. Babe quickly made a name for himself on the Orioles, dazzling fans and teammates alike with his pitching prowess. His fastball was like a bolt of lightning—quick, powerful, and a little bit scary if you were on the receiving end. He also started to showcase his batting skills, which, let's be honest, were nothing short of magical. It didn't take long for the big leagues to notice. In fact, his talent was so undeniable that Jack Dunn had no choice but to sell Babe's contract to the Boston Red Sox later that same year, 1914.

Here's the scene: a bustling Boston, with its cobblestone streets and lively crowds, where the Sox fans were known for their passion (and occasional bouts of overzealous enthusiasm). Babe Ruth, barely out of his teens, found himself amidst the excitement and pressure of Major League Baseball. He made his debut as a pitcher, and did he make an impression! He finished his first season with the Red Sox with a respectable record, showing everyone that he was not just a flash in the pan.

But 1915 was where things started to get really interesting. Babe was not just a good pitcher; he was a phenomenal one. He pitched in 32 games, won 18 of them, and maintained an earned run average (ERA) that would make any pitcher green with envy. And let's not forget his batting. Even though pitchers didn't usually bat much back then, Babe had a habit of smashing the ball out of the park whenever he got the chance. His teammates couldn't help but notice that this big guy with a big heart and an even bigger swing was something special.

As the seasons rolled by, Babe Ruth's legend began to grow. By 1916, he was one of the top pitchers in the league. He led the American League with nine shutouts—a record that stands out even today. And if you're wondering what a shutout is, it's when a pitcher doesn't allow the opposing team to score any runs during the entire game. Think about throwing the ball so well that not a single player from the other team can even dream of reaching home plate—that was Babe Ruth. And here's a fun fact: Babe Ruth loved to experiment. He wasn't satisfied with being an outstanding pitcher. No, sir. He wanted to hit, and hit hard. His batting practice sessions became legendary. Coaches and players would gather around to watch Babe launch baseballs into the stratosphere, each swing accompanied by a collective gasp and the occasional clatter of a broken window somewhere in the distance. His home run prowess began to overshadow his pitching, and the Red Sox started to take notice.

In 1918, the world was in a bit of chaos—there was a war going on (World War I), after all—but baseball provided a much-needed distraction. That year, Babe Ruth became a dual threat, playing more as a position player while still pitching occasionally. He hit 11 home runs, leading the league, and played a significant role in helping the Red Sox win the World Series. Babe's versatility was nothing short of revolutionary. It's like a player today who is the best pitcher and one of the best hitters at the same time—it's almost unimaginable!

But it was 1919 that really marked the turning point in Babe Ruth's career. He set a new single-season home run record by smashing 29 homers, a feat that left fans and fellow players in awe. It was clear that Babe had outgrown his role as a pitcher. His batting skills were too extraordinary to be limited to just the occasional at-bat. The Red Sox had a decision to make: continue to use Babe as a pitcher or unleash his full potential as a hitter. Spoiler alert—they chose the latter.

However, the winds of change were blowing. The Red Sox owner, Harry Frazee, made a decision that would go down in baseball infamy. In December 1919, he sold Babe Ruth to the New York Yankees. The exact reasons are still debated, but let's just say it had a bit to do with finances and a whole lot to do with a certain Broadway play Frazee wanted to finance. This moment is often referred to as the "Curse of the Bambino" because, after the sale, the Red Sox didn't win another World Series for 86 years. Ouch!

So, there you have it—Babe Ruth, the young firecracker from Baltimore, had not only become a superstar with the Boston Red Sox but was now on his way to New York City, ready to set the baseball world on fire. He was no longer only a talented player; he was on the brink of becoming a legend.

So, Babe Ruth's journey with the Boston Red Sox had come to a dramatic, almost theatrical end, and now he was heading to the Big Apple—the city that never sleeps, home of skyscrapers, jazz, and, of course, the New York Yankees!

Like in a Hollywood movie, there was Babe stepping off the train in New York City in 1920, the city's energy buzzing around him, skyscrapers towering overhead like giants in a fairy tale. Babe joined the Yankees, but he also transformed them. Up until then, the Yankees had never won a World Series. They were like the underdog in a sports movie—full of heart but always coming up short. But with Babe on the team, everything changed. In his first season with the Yankees, he hit a mind-boggling 54 home runs—yes, 54! That was more than most entire teams managed to hit. Yankee Stadium quickly earned the nickname "The House That Ruth Built" because Babe's incredible popularity and on-field heroics were the driving force behind the stadium's construction.

Let's also talk about Yankee Stadium. Opening in 1923, it was a baseball cathedral, and Babe Ruth was its main attraction. The stadium could hold 58,000 fans, and it often seemed like every single seat was filled whenever Babe stepped up to the plate. The roar of the crowd when Babe swung his mighty bat must have been deafening—like a thunderstorm of cheers. Babe's batting was nothing short of legendary. He had a unique swing, a combination of brute strength and uncanny precision. It was as if he could see into the future, knowing exactly where the ball would be before it even left the pitcher's hand. And those home runs! Each one was an event, a spectacle that drew gasps and cheers. They called him the Colossus of Clout for a reason!

Babe's personality was larger than life. He was the life of the party—always up for a laugh, a joke, and a good time. He had an insatiable appetite for hot dogs, soda, and, well, pretty much everything! Babe Ruth loved life, and life loved him back. He was more than a baseball player; he was a cultural icon, a symbol of the exuberance and optimism of the Roaring Twenties—a decade when jazz filled the air, people celebrated newfound prosperity, and innovations like cars and radios brought excitement to everyday life. Babe's escapades off the field were as legendary as his feats on it. Stories of his larger-than-life appetite for food, drink, and adventure spread far and wide, making him a household name even among those who never watched a single game of baseball.

The 1920s were a golden era for Babe and the Yankees. In 1921, Babe broke his own home run record by hitting 59 dingers. Just think about that—a baseball flying out of the park almost 60 times in a single season! The Yankees rode Babe's powerful swing all the way to their first American League pennant. Though they lost the World Series to the New York Giants, the stage was set for a dynasty.

And then came 1923, a year that would forever be etched in baseball lore. Babe led the Yankees to their first World Series title, defeating the Giants. It was a triumph that cemented his status as the greatest player in the game. The 1923 season was also memorable because it was the year Yankee Stadium opened, with Babe hitting a home run on the very first day—talk about making an entrance!

But Babe continued making history. In 1927, he and the Yankees put together what many still consider the greatest baseball team of all time. Known as "Murderers' Row," the lineup was filled with power hitters, but none more fearsome than Babe Ruth. That year, Babe set a new single-season home run record by hitting 60 homers—a mark that stood for 34 years. The Yankees dominated the league and swept the Pittsburgh Pirates in the World Series.

Babe Ruth's impact wasn't limited to his prodigious home runs. He was a showman who understood the value of entertainment. He'd call his shots, pointing to the stands before smashing a home run to that exact spot (or so the stories go). He was the king of the ballpark, and fans flocked to see him play and witness his greatness firsthand. And while Babe was a giant on the field, he also had a heart of gold. He often visited children in hospitals, bringing them gifts and a much-needed dose of joy. He loved kids and made it a point to be a positive role model, despite his own sometimes rowdy behavior. There are countless stories of Babe's generosity—like the time he paid for a child's operation or the many times he handed out signed baseballs to fans. Babe Ruth was a baseball player and a hero to many.

In the 1930s, Babe continued to put up impressive numbers even as he got older. He was a bit like a superhero whose powers never seemed to fade. He helped the Yankees win more championships, further solidifying their place as baseball royalty. Babe's presence in the lineup was a guarantee of excitement, and every at-bat was a must-see event. He continued to break records and set new standards for what it meant to be a baseball superstar.

Babe Ruth left an indelible mark on the game of baseball. He was a pioneer who changed the way the game was played and perceived. His incredible feats on the field and his larger-than-life personality made him a legend in his own time and for generations to come. The kid from Baltimore who found his calling on the baseball diamond became a hero in Boston and then went on to build a dynasty in New York. His journey from the sandlots of Baltimore to the grandeur of Yankee Stadium is a tale of talent, determination, and an undeniable love for the game of baseball.

Jackie Robinson

Breaking Barriers

Gather 'round, everyone, and let me tell you about a guy named Jackie Robinson. Born on January 31, 1919, in a place called Cairo, Georgia—not Egypt, mind you; this Cairo had more peanuts than pyramids—Jackie entered the world as the youngest of five siblings. His parents were Mallie and Jerry Robinson. But life in Georgia was no peach, so after Jackie's dad left, his mom packed up the family and moved to sunny California, specifically Pasadena. California was like a whole new ballgame compared to Georgia. The Robinsons settled into a neighborhood where Jackie grew up running around, probably imagining he was a wild stallion, and that was just the beginning of his legendary speed.

Jackie's feet were like jet engines, and he learned new sports as quickly as a magician pulling rabbits out of a hat. By the time he reached John Muir High School, Jackie was practically a one-man band of athletes. He played football, basketball, track, and baseball. Picking between those sports is like deciding between pizza and a burger—both are awesome, but why choose when you can have both? Well, Jackie didn't choose; he played them all and played them well.

Speaking of playing well, let's chat about one of his buddies at Muir High, a guy named Carl Anderson. Carl was pretty much Jackie's partner in crime (the good kind). They'd challenge each other, pushing to new athletic heights, and if sports were a superhero team, these two would be Batman and Robin, swooping in to save the day with touchdowns and home runs. High school ended, but Jackie's talent didn't. He zipped over to Pasadena Junior College, and guess what? More sports! At PJC, Jackie wasn't content with being a mere mortal athlete. Nope, he was a beast on the field, particularly in football and baseball. He set school records in track and was making everyone else look like they were moving in slow motion. One memorable moment was during a baseball game where he stole home. Stealing home is like trying to swipe a cookie from the jar right under your mom's nose—it's bold, risky, and if you pull it off, you feel like the coolest kid ever.

After dazzling everyone at PJC, Jackie took his talents to the University of California, Los Angeles (UCLA). He became the first student to earn varsity letters in four sports—football, basketball, track, and baseball. Seriously, if someone invented underwater basket weaving, Jackie probably would've lettered in that too. But life had its fair share of rainy days and fumbles. UCLA was also where Jackie met his future wife, Rachel Isum, and though that's another chapter for later, just know she was a rock in his life.

But college couldn't contain Jackie's talent forever. In 1941, he left UCLA just short of graduation. The world outside had a lot going on, including a little thing called World War II. Jackie enlisted in the Army, and here's where things get more intense than a high-stakes game in the ninth inning. He was assigned to a segregated unit—segregation in the military was like having two teams, and one gets all the good equipment while the other gets whatever's left. Jackie had a knack for getting on his feet and tackling unfairness head-on. In 1944, stationed at Fort Hood in Texas, he faced a court-martial for refusing to move to the back of an Army bus. Not easy when you're being told to sit at the back of the bus when you know you've got every right to sit anywhere you like. Jackie stood up for himself, was arrested, and subsequently acquitted of all charges. This was no small potatoes; it was like hitting a grand slam in a stadium that didn't want you to play.

When the war ended, Jackie was honorably discharged and went back to civilian life. The Kansas City Monarchs of the Negro Leagues came calling, and in 1945, Jackie signed on. Playing in the Negro Leagues was like being in an exclusive club of incredibly talented players who, because of the color line in baseball, weren't allowed in the Major Leagues. Interestingly, before the color barrier was established, baseball had seen Black players like Moses Fleetwood Walker in the late 1800s. But segregationist policies had enforced a strict separation, pushing Black players out of white leagues. The Monarchs traveled a lot, playing ball and showing the country what real talent looked like.

Jackie Robinson's journey with the Kansas City Monarchs in 1945 is part of a bigger story about how baseball used to be split up. Back then, Black players weren't allowed to play in the same leagues as white players because of something called the "color line," a rule that was unfair and had been around since the 1800s. So, Black players created their own leagues, called the Negro Leagues, and the games were packed with excitement! In fact, some of those games were so awesome that even more fans showed up than at Major League games—sometimes as many as 40,000 people!

While playing for the Monarchs, Jackie faced tough challenges, like long, tiring trips and segregation, which meant people were unfairly separated because of the color of their skin. But despite all that, Jackie played so well that he got noticed by Branch Rickey, the boss of the Brooklyn Dodgers. Rickey had a big idea: he wanted to bring Black players into Major League Baseball. Some people think he did this because he wanted to change things for the better, but Rickey also knew how talented these players were and how many new fans they could bring to the game.

In August 1945, Jackie had a famous meeting with Rickey. Rickey wanted to make sure Jackie was ready for all the tough stuff he'd face as the first Black player in Major League Baseball. He said something that really stuck: "I need a man who has the guts not to fight back." Jackie agreed because he knew he was fighting for something bigger than just himself.

A couple of months later, in October 1945, Jackie signed with the Montreal Royals, a minor league team for the Dodgers. This was a huge deal! It was the beginning of a big change in baseball and in America. When Jackie finally joined the Dodgers in 1947, he broke the "color barrier" and opened the door for many other Black players to follow their dreams, even though the Negro Leagues started to fade away. But Jackie's success was just the beginning of a brand-new chapter for baseball!

So there Jackie was, ready to step into a world that was anything but ready for him. The year was 1946, and Jackie Robinson took the field for the Montreal Royals, the Brooklyn Dodgers' top minor league team. Here we are, a sea of fans, eyes wide and skeptical, watching as Jackie Robinson, the first Black player in the International League, ran onto the field. It was like stepping onto another planet where the gravity was heavier and the air was thicker, but Jackie didn't miss a beat.

From his very first game, Jackie was a sensation. In his debut, he hit a three-run home run, as if to say, "Get ready, world, I'm here to play." That season, Jackie led the league with a .349 batting average and scored an incredible 113 runs. But those stats were only part of the story. What about trying to play baseball while carrying the weight of an entire race's hopes and dreams on your shoulders? Tough, right? Yet Jackie did it with a mix of grace and determination that left everyone in awe, whether they wanted to admit it or not.

But the path wasn't lined with roses. Jackie faced hostility from fans and even fellow players. Opposing teams hurled insults, some players spiked him intentionally, and pitchers threw at him more often than was normal. It was like Jackie had a bullseye on his back. Yet, he managed to dodge and weave through these challenges, keeping his cool when many would have snapped. Then came April 15, 1947. Mark that date because it's the day baseball—and America—changed forever.

On April 15, 1947, the Brooklyn Dodgers called Jackie up to the major leagues. Ebbets Field was packed, buzzing with anticipation and tension. Jackie Robinson, wearing number 42, trotted onto the field. The Dodgers' manager, Leo Durocher, had Jackie's back, famously declaring, "I don't care if the guy is yellow or black, or if he has stripes like a zebra. I'm the manager of this team, and I say he plays." Jackie's entrance into the major leagues was a mixed bag; he didn't get a hit in his debut, yet he scored a run, and his presence alone was groundbreaking. The crowd was a mix of supporters and skeptics, but as the season progressed, Jackie's extraordinary talent began to speak louder than any words. He batted .297, led the league in stolen bases, and was named Rookie of the Year. Put yourself in his shoes—every game a battle, every hit a statement, every stolen base a silent scream of defiance and triumph.

Yet the pressure-cooker environment didn't let up. Some teammates were initially hesitant to play alongside him. Pee Wee Reese, the Dodgers' captain, famously put an arm around Jackie on the field—a simple gesture that spoke volumes. It was like a beacon of humanity, cutting through a fog of prejudice. This moment was about showing that fairness and friendship could exist even in the toughest of times. On the road, things were often even tougher. There were hotels that wouldn't let Jackie stay with the team, restaurants that refused to serve him. Imagine traveling with your team and then being told you can't stay in the same place or eat with them because of your skin color. But Jackie didn't let these indignities derail him. He used them as fuel, channeling his frustration into his game, turning obstacles into stepping stones.

One of the most intense episodes happened in 1947 during a series against the Philadelphia Phillies. Ben Chapman, the Phillies' manager, led his team in a barrage of racist taunts. It was ugly—a stark reminder of the hatred Jackie was up against. Yet, he kept his composure, proving he had both physical prowess and mental toughness. This incident caused a media frenzy, and even though it was a dark moment, it forced many people to confront their own prejudices.

Jackie's second season in 1948 was another triumph. His batting average climbed to .296, and he continued to steal bases with a cunning and speed that left opponents in the dust. He was shaking up baseball culture, far more than racking up stats and trophies. He showed that excellence on the field couldn't be ignored, no matter how much some people wanted to keep things "the way they were." His success forced baseball—and America—to look in the mirror and see the absurdity of segregation. Teammates who once doubted him began to see the bigger picture. Duke Snider, a Dodgers outfielder, reflected years later on how Jackie's courage and skill changed minds and hearts. The locker room began to feel different, too—less about division and more about unity, thanks to the barrier Jackie broke through sheer willpower and talent.

So, by the end of the 1940s, Jackie Robinson was more than a baseball player. He was a symbol of progress, a living testament to what could be achieved when talent met opportunity. He'd faced down racism, hostility, and doubt, emerging not just as a great player but as a great man.

Let's dive right back into the action, shall we? It's the late 1940s, and Jackie Robinson is smashing barriers to smithereens. Every time he steps onto the field, it's like watching a master artist at work, and the canvas is that glorious diamond of dirt and grass. By the time we hit 1949, Jackie is a full-blown superstar, and it's hard to overstate his impact.

1949, folks—what a year! Jackie won the National League MVP Award, a tremendous feat that confirmed what everyone who watched him already knew: he was one of the best to ever play the game. He batted a scorching .342, drove in 124 runs, and stole 37 bases. Let's put this in perspective: stealing a base in baseball is like trying to snatch candy from a jar while everyone's watching—you need speed, cunning, and nerves of steel. Jackie had all of that in spades.

But his influence went beyond stats and awards. Jackie was altering the way people viewed race and talent in America. He was playing a pivotal role in the Civil Rights Movement. Every time Jackie stole a base or hit a home run, it was like a challenge to the segregationists. It was more than baseball; it was a statement. Jackie's 1950 season saw him maintaining his peak form, hitting .328 with 99 RBIs. The Dodgers were riding high, and much of that success was thanks to Jackie's electrifying play. Off the field, Jackie was as active as ever, speaking out against racial injustice and using his growing platform to advocate for equality. He was like a beacon of hope for countless Americans, proving that change was possible through talent, resilience, and sheer determination.

1951 rolled around, and Jackie's momentum didn't falter. His batting average stayed strong, and he continued to be a nightmare for pitchers and catchers alike with his aggressive base running. However, 1951 was also marked by a fierce rivalry with the New York Giants, culminating in one of the most famous moments in baseball history: Bobby

Thomson's "Shot Heard 'Round the World." The Dodgers lost the pennant in a dramatic playoff, but even in defeat, Jackie's performance was stellar.

Moving into 1952, Jackie faced physical challenges. Years of playing all-out were taking a toll on his body, but his spirit was as unbreakable as ever. He adapted his game, focusing more on his hitting and less on his aggressive base running. And yet, he still managed to steal 24 bases and hit .308. It's like watching a superhero who, even when they're slightly wounded, still manages to save the day repeatedly. 1953 and 1954 were solid years for Jackie. His leadership on the field was invaluable, and he played multiple positions, showing his versatility. This adaptability was one of Jackie's greatest strengths. He was like a Swiss Army knife—always ready for whatever challenge came his way, whether that meant playing second base, first base, or even the outfield.

Then came 1955, the year the Brooklyn Dodgers finally captured the World Series title. After years of "close but no cigar" moments, they toppled the mighty New York Yankees in seven games. Jackie's performance was crucial, as always. Though his batting average in the Series wasn't eye-popping, his presence and leadership were instrumental in the Dodgers' victory. It was like seeing a long, arduous journey come to a joyous conclusion. The victory parade was a testament to how far Jackie and the team had come.

1956 was Jackie's final year in the majors. He batted .275, not quite his previous heights but still respectable. More importantly, he continued to inspire both on and off the field. His career was winding down, but his influence was ramping up. Jackie's fight against discrimination didn't end when the final out was made. He continued to be a powerful voice for civil rights and social justice.

So, let's recap some of the peaks and highlights of Jackie's astonishing career:

- **Breaking the Color Barrier (1947)**: Jackie's entry into Major League Baseball—a personal and national milestone.

- **1949 MVP Award**: His .342 batting average, 124 RBIs, and 37 stolen bases made this a banner year.

- **World Series Champion (1955)**: The Dodgers' victory was a culmination of years of effort, with Jackie at the heart of it all.

- **Versatility**: Whether playing second base, first base, or the outfield, Jackie's adaptability showcased his exceptional talent and intelligence on the field.

- **Civil Rights Advocacy**: Off the field, Jackie's commitment to equality and justice remained unwavering, making him a true hero beyond the baseball diamond.

By the time Jackie hung up his cleats, he had transformed the game of baseball and also the social fabric of America. His courage, skill, and determination paved the way for countless others, proving that talent knows no color and that the human spirit can overcome even the most entrenched barriers. He was an athlete and a pioneer, a warrior and a beacon of hope. His legacy on the field—filled with dazzling plays, clutch hits, and stolen bases—was matched by his off-field impact. Every time we celebrate a great baseball moment today, a part of that celebration is a nod to Jackie, the man who changed the game and the nation forever.

Willie Mays

The Say Hey Kid

Let's hit a home run right from the get-go! It's the early 1940s, and a young boy named Willie Mays is darting around the dusty fields of Westfield, Alabama, like he's got a turbo boost installed in his sneakers. This kid is lightning fast. We're talking about the kind of speed that makes cheetahs consider second careers as house cats. Born on May 6, 1931, Willie Mays grew up in a tight-knit community, where everyone knew everyone, and if they didn't, well, they'd know about it by dinner time.

Willie was surrounded by baseball practically from the cradle. His father, Willie Sr., known affectionately as "Kitty Cat," played semi-pro baseball, and his mother, Annie, was a gifted athlete in her own right. It's like they brewed up a perfect genetic potion for athleticism. Baby Willie would be clutching a baseball before he even figured out how to walk. While other toddlers were playing with building blocks, Willie was probably strategizing his first steal.

Westfield was no big city. It was a small, industrial town that lived and breathed the rhythms of the steel mill where most folks worked. But when the workday ended and the sun started to set, that's when the magic happened. The local baseball field, a patchy green oasis amidst the gritty landscape, became the center of the universe. Here, Willie watched his dad and other local legends swing bats, pitch balls, and engage in the kind of animated banter that could rival a flock of gossiping geese.

Young Willie, with his big, curious eyes, soaked it all up like a sponge. His father taught him the fundamentals, but it was little Willie's unquenchable thirst for the game that set him apart. By the age of ten, he could run faster, throw farther, and hit harder than kids twice his age. Not to mention, his infectious enthusiasm made him the heart and soul of every sandlot game—a pint-sized dynamo sprinting around bases, outmaneuvering kids left and right, with a grin as wide as a baseball glove.

Middle school came and went, with Willie leaving a trail of awestruck spectators in his wake. By the time he entered Fairfield Industrial High School, Willie Mays had already cemented his reputation as a local phenom. It wasn't long before he was playing not just for the high school team but also for the Birmingham Black Barons of the Negro American League. Think of being in high school and also playing professional baseball—that's like being a superhero by day and an even bigger superhero by night.

Balancing school and a burgeoning baseball career was no easy feat. One minute, Willie is scribbling down algebra equations (probably faster than anyone else in the class), and the next, he's hopping on a bus to play against seasoned veterans who probably used chewing tobacco as breakfast cereal. But Willie thrived on it. His incredible work ethic, fueled by an unyielding passion for the game, allowed him to juggle these dual roles with an ease that left everyone around him baffled.

The Birmingham Black Barons were no slouches. They were a powerhouse in the Negro Leagues, and playing for them meant that Willie faced off against some of the most formidable players in baseball history. Despite his young age, Willie didn't flinch. He held his own, showcasing the same electric energy and jaw-dropping skills that would later make him a household name. He was that teenager stepping up to the plate, his eyes narrowing as he focused on the pitcher, the crowd holding its breath, and then—wham! The ball soars through the air, and Willie is off, rounding the bases like a human blur.

But let's not forget the social context of the time. This was the 1940s, a period marked by racial segregation and profound inequalities. Playing in the Negro Leagues, Willie experienced the harsh realities of discrimination firsthand. Yet, instead of dampening his spirit, these challenges only fueled his determination. He was determined not just to play the game but to change it, to be a beacon of hope and excellence for others.

Now, imagine being one of his high school classmates. You're sitting in geometry class, struggling to figure out the area of a triangle, and there's Willie Mays, who can not only solve the problem but probably calculate the trajectory of a baseball mid-flight. Teachers found it both amusing and challenging to keep Willie grounded in academics when his heart and mind were constantly on the diamond. Yet, he remained a good student, respectful and diligent, knowing that his education was just as important as his athletic dreams.

So, you've got it—a whirlwind tour of Willie's early years. From the dirt fields of Westfield to the professional stadiums of the Negro Leagues, his journey is nothing short of extraordinary. His early life was a heady mix of boundless energy, incredible talent, and a community that nurtured his dreams. As we stand on the threshold of the next phase of his life, one thing is crystal clear: the world had only begun to witness the magic of the Say Hey Kid!

So we left off with young Willie dazzling everyone from the sandlots of Westfield to the professional fields of the Birmingham Black Barons. But this was only the beginning. The next chapter in Willie Mays's life story is where things get even more electrifying—think fireworks, but with baseballs. In 1950, Willie signed with the New York Giants, who sent him to their minor league team, the Trenton Giants. Moving from Alabama to New Jersey might seem like going from a cozy small town to the bustling East Coast. But did he mind? He took it all in stride. After all, this was the guy who hitched rides with seasoned players as a teenager and balanced algebra with base-stealing. A new state was merely another base to round.

Playing for the Trenton Giants in the Class B Interstate League, Willie immediately stood out. The moment he stepped onto the field, his youthful energy electrified the air. His batting average soared to .353, and his outfield plays left everyone in awe. It's like a gazelle combined with a hawk—swift, agile, and always precise. That's Willie in the outfield. Spectators quickly realized they were witnessing something special, like spotting a shooting star on a clear night.

But let's not skip over the colorful details of minor league life. The travel was grueling, the accommodations far from luxurious, and the paychecks were smaller than a peanut. Yet, Willie thrived. He had this uncanny ability to turn adversity into motivation. Long bus rides? More time to mentally rehearse his game. Sparse lodgings? Just a place to dream about future home runs. And those meager paychecks? Well, they were a small price to pay for the love of the game.

In 1951, Willie was promoted to the Minneapolis Millers, a Class AAA team. This was the final stop before hitting the major leagues, and he hit the ground running—literally. Minneapolis fans were treated to a show as Willie batted .477 over 35 games. Yep, you read that right—.477! It was like he had a magnet in his bat and the ball was made of iron. His speed, his bat, his glove—it all came together in a performance that screamed, "Get this guy to the majors!" And so, the call came. On May 24, 1951, he made his debut with the New York Giants.

The iconic Polo Grounds were packed with fans, buzzing with anticipation. The Giants were in a slump, and they needed a spark, something—or someone—to reignite their fire. Willie stepped onto the field, and though his initial at-bats didn't set the world ablaze (he went 0-for-12 to start), there was an unmistakable aura about him, the kind that makes you nudge your buddy and say, "Keep an eye on this kid."

Then, on May 28, 1951, he got his first major league hit—a towering home run off the great Warren Spahn. It was as if the baseball gods themselves decided to let everyone know that Willie Mays had arrived. That home run was a harbinger of the spectacular career to come. Willie's bat cracked like thunder, and from that moment on, there was no looking back.

His rookie season was a mix of ups and downs, as all great stories are. He struggled initially but finished with a respectable .274 average, hitting 20 home runs and earning the National League Rookie of the Year award. But the stats alone don't tell the full story. Willie brought an exuberance to the game, a joy that was contagious. Teammates, opponents, fans—everyone felt it. He played as if every game were his first, with a mix of awe and unbridled enthusiasm that made even the most jaded spectator believe in the magic of baseball.

The 1951 season also featured one of the most dramatic moments in baseball history—Bobby Thomson's "Shot Heard 'Round the World." The Giants were locked in a fierce pennant race with the Brooklyn Dodgers, and it all came down to a three-game playoff. Willie was on deck when Thomson hit the legendary home run to win the pennant for the Giants. The Polo Grounds were in a frenzy, players mobbing Thomson at home plate, and there's Willie, a mix of jubilation and a sense of destiny written on his face. It was the perfect prelude to the stardom that awaited him.

As Willie settled into his role with the Giants, his impact on the field became more pronounced. His fielding prowess earned him the nickname "The Say Hey Kid," a nod to his youthful exuberance and the cheerful way he'd call out to teammates with a friendly "Say hey!"

His basket catches, where he'd nonchalantly snag fly balls at waist level, became his trademark. Fans loved it; opponents feared it. There was an element of showmanship, sure, but also an undeniable skill that made these plays look effortless.

So, from the fields of Alabama to the Polo Grounds Stadium, Willie Mays's rise was meteoric, filled with the kind of grit, talent, and charisma that legends are made of. The minor leagues tested him, but he passed with flying colors, and his major league debut set the stage for one of the most remarkable careers in sports history. The world had seen the early brilliance of Willie Mays, but the best was yet to come.

We're about to launch into the stratosphere with Willie Mays during his peak years. This is where legends are made. Willie Mays in the 1950s and '60s—a time when baseball reigned supreme, and every kid wanted to be like Willie—the hero with a heart as big as his talent.

It's 1954, and Willie Mays is back from serving in the U.S. Army, ready to make his mark. That year, the New York Giants were on a mission, and Willie was their guiding star. The highlight? The World Series against the Cleveland Indians. At this point, if you've ever seen a baseball highlight reel, you know where I'm headed. The play that's become synonymous with Mays: "The Catch."

The Polo Grounds were packed with fans, tension so thick you could cut it with a knife. Vic Wertz smashes a ball deep into center field, and everyone thinks it's a sure hit. But wait! Willie turns, sprints toward the deepest part of the park, and with his back to the plate, he makes an over-the-shoulder catch that defies the laws of physics. It's like he borrowed some of Superman's powers for the afternoon. He whirls and fires the ball back to the infield, preventing the runners from advancing. The crowd erupts, and in that moment, Willie Mays is a legend in the making.

That catch wasn't a fluke; it was the epitome of Mays's career—grace under pressure, astounding athleticism, and an uncanny baseball IQ. The Giants went on to sweep the Indians, and Willie's contribution was invaluable. His performance that year earned him the National League MVP, batting .345 with 41 home runs and 110 RBIs. He led the league in batting average, slugging percentage, and total bases. Essentially, he was a one-man wrecking crew, dismantling opponents with a blend of power and finesse.

The years that followed saw Willie Mays consistently dominating the league. He wasn't just playing baseball; he was redefining it. In 1955, he hit 51 home runs, leading the league and establishing himself as a force to be reckoned with. His enthusiasm for the game was infectious, and he had a knack for making the extraordinary look routine. Diving catches, towering home runs, lightning-fast base running—Mays did it all, often with a playful smile that made it look as though he was having more fun than anyone else on the field.

Then came 1957, a year that underscored his defensive genius. Willie won his first of twelve consecutive Gold Glove Awards. That's right—twelve! It's as if every year, the glove committee saw the competition, shrugged, and said, "Just give it to Mays." His basket catches became his signature move, an iconic style that kids across America tried to emulate, often with hilarious results (imagine a bunch of kids flubbing fly balls in backyards while yelling, "Say hey!").

By 1958, the Giants had relocated to San Francisco, and Willie's talent helped ease the team's transition to the West Coast. Candlestick Park became his new playground, and he quickly won over fans with his electrifying play. In 1962, he led the Giants to the World Series again, though they fell to the New York Yankees in a hard-fought series. That season, Willie had 49 home runs and 141 RBIs, showcasing his remarkable consistency and power.

One of the most mind-boggling stats from his career is his 660 home runs. But it's not just the number—it's how he hit them. He could blast them to any part of the park, off any pitcher, in any situation. And let's not forget his 338 stolen bases. Willie was a five-tool player in the truest sense, excelling in hitting for average, hitting for power, base running, throwing, and fielding. It was like having five players rolled into one, each aspect of his game a masterclass.

The 1960s were a golden era for Mays. In 1965, he hit 52 home runs, won another MVP, and continued to astound with his defensive wizardry. He was named to 24 All-Star teams over his career, a testament to his enduring excellence and popularity. Fans would pack stadiums for a chance to see Willie play, knowing they were witnessing history every time he took the field.

And even off the field, Mays was a big figure. His charisma, humility, and genuine love for the game made him a beloved figure in San Francisco and across the country. He was friends with celebrities, appeared on television shows, and his star power transcended baseball. Yet, despite all the adulation, Willie remained grounded, never losing sight of the joy that baseball brought him and countless fans.

By the late 1960s and early 1970s, even as age started to catch up with him, Mays continued to play at a high level. His knowledge of the game, his instinctual brilliance, allowed him to outthink younger, physically stronger players. Watching Mays in these years was like watching a grandmaster at chess—every move calculated, every swing a stroke of genius.

In 1972, he returned to New York with the Mets, providing fans with a nostalgic encore of his greatness. Though his playing time was limited, his impact was immeasurable, mentoring younger players and delighting fans who cherished seeing him in action one last time.

The peak years of Willie Mays marked a time when he transformed from a promising young player into one of the greatest to ever play the game. His career was a symphony of athletic prowess, strategic brilliance, and sheer joy. Willie Mays didn't just play baseball; he elevated it, creating a legacy that resonates through the ages. Every catch, every home run, every stolen base was a testament to his dedication and unparalleled talent.

Hank Aaron

Chasing the Dream

Let's kick things off in Mobile, Alabama, on February 5, 1934, when the universe decided it needed a little more spice and delivered Henry Louis "Hank" Aaron into the world—a tiny, scrappy baby with an unshakable determination to become one of baseball's greatest hitters ever. But, of course, no one knew that yet. At the time, they were probably more concerned with the fact that he cried like a banshee and ate like he was training for an eating contest.

Growing up in the midst of the Great Depression, young Hank found life far from easy. His family lived in a modest home in the Toulminville neighborhood of Mobile, Alabama, a working-class area that could make the term "humble beginnings" sound like a luxury resort. Hank's father, Herbert, worked various odd jobs to make ends meet, while his mother, Estella, managed the household and their eight children. Yes, you read that right—eight children. If you think your family dinners are chaotic, imagine the Aaron household!

Amidst this bustling family life, young Hank found solace in baseball. Despite the financial challenges, he didn't sit around moping. Instead, he developed an early love for the game. Back then, baseball was an escape, a dream factory. Hank's dream factory was the local sandlots and vacant lots where he played baseball with friends. These places were far from your average baseball diamonds; more like dusty patches of earth with makeshift bases. But for Hank and his friends, they might as well have been Yankee Stadium.

Hank didn't have a proper bat or glove, so he made do with what he had. Using sticks as bats and rag balls made from materials found around the neighborhood, he honed his skills. It might sound like a scene out of a quirky sports movie, but it really happened. Excelling with improvised equipment sharpened his hand-eye coordination, making hitting a real baseball seem almost effortless. Despite the lack of proper gear, Hank made it work. Swinging that broomstick with a fire in his eyes that could melt steel, he was a kid with a heart full of dreams and pockets full of nothing. It was clear from a young age that Hank had something special—not just talent, but also grit, determination, and a love for the game that burned brighter than the Alabama sun.

As he grew older, his passion for baseball only intensified. By the time he was a teenager, Hank was playing for the Mobile Black Bears, a local team that gave him his first taste of organized baseball. Playing with the Black Bears was a big deal for Hank. Not only did it provide him with more experience, but it also exposed him to better competition and, most importantly, scouts.

While Hank's time with the Black Bears showcased his talent, he faced significant challenges off the field. The South in the 1940s and 1950s was steeped in racial segregation, and for a young African American like Hank, discrimination was a harsh reality. These experiences, while difficult, fueled his determination to succeed rather than breaking his spirit. One of the most remarkable things about Hank's early years was his ability to stay focused on his goals despite the obstacles. Whether dealing with racism or the everyday struggles of growing up poor, Hank's resilience was unwavering. He didn't let negativity or hardship knock him off course. If anything, they pushed him to work harder, to prove that he belonged on the field as a player and a star.

During his time with the Black Bears, Hank's talent didn't go unnoticed. Scouts were impressed by his natural ability and exceptional hand-eye coordination. In 1952, Hank joined the Indianapolis Clowns of the Negro American League, marking his transition from a local hero to a national talent. The Indianapolis Clowns were among the most prominent teams in the Negro Leagues, known for both their entertainment value and competitive play. They didn't recruit players who couldn't hold their own, and Hank quickly proved he was more than capable. Playing shortstop and outfield, he showcased his versatility and athleticism. With the Clowns, Hank's reputation began to grow. He was known for his incredible hitting ability, his speed, and his cool, composed demeanor on the field.

His performance was spectacular, hitting .366 and attracting the attention of Major League scouts. His time there was brief but impactful, serving as a springboard to the Major Leagues. Through it all, Hank never lost sight of where he came from. Despite his early fame and the growing attention, he remained grounded. His family and the lessons he learned growing up in Mobile stayed with him. They shaped his character and his approach to the game. Hank knew that talent could take you far, but hard work and determination made the difference. The early years of Hank Aaron were filled with makeshift bats, rag balls, and a relentless pursuit of a dream. From the dusty fields of Carver Park to the semi-pro diamonds with the Mobile Black Bears, Hank's journey was just beginning. The challenges he faced and the perseverance he showed would become the foundation for his legendary career in baseball.

After showcasing his impressive skills with the Indianapolis Clowns, Hank Aaron was ready for the next big step in his baseball journey. His performance caused a frenzy among Major League Baseball scouts, who saw in Hank a potential game-changer. Among them were representatives from the Boston Braves, eager to add serious talent to their roster. Thus began Hank's ascent through the Minor Leagues—a crucial chapter in his story before reaching the Majors.

In 1952, Hank signed a contract with the Boston Braves' organization, which assigned him to their farm team, the Eau Claire Bears in Wisconsin. Imagine going from the sweltering heat of Mobile, Alabama, to the chilly breezes of the Midwest—quite the climate shock. But Hank, being the adaptable person he was, didn't let that faze him. He was focused on proving himself, no matter where he played.

At Eau Claire, Hank didn't just prove himself; he practically rewrote the rulebook on rookie success. He batted .336, showcasing his batting prowess, and earned the Northern League Rookie of the Year award. His fielding, though not yet as polished as his batting, showed promise and versatility. Playing as an infielder and outfielder, Hank demonstrated that he was a jack-of-all-trades, ready to master any position. His teammates and coaches saw a young player with an old soul's work ethic—a combination that promised a bright future.

Hank's success in Eau Claire was a clear signal that he was ready for the next challenge. Moving to the Jacksonville Braves in 1953 was significant for Hank. Not only was it a step closer to the Major Leagues, but it also made him one of the first African American players in the South Atlantic League, a league notorious for its racial segregation.

In the early 1950s, the South Atlantic League was a challenging environment for African American players. Hank faced racism and hostility from fans and opposing players alike. Yet, he refused to let these obstacles deter him. Instead, he let his performance speak volumes. Batting .362, he led the league in runs, hits, doubles, and RBIs, earning the league's MVP award. His outstanding play served as a beacon, breaking through the racial barriers that sought to hold him back.

Despite the obstacles, Hank's time in Jacksonville was transformative. He learned to handle pressure with grace, to let his bat do the talking, and to stay focused on his goals no matter what. His resilience earned him the respect of his teammates and even some of his opponents. Jacksonville was a tough battleground, but it was also a proving ground that shaped Hank into a player who could handle anything.

After his season with the Jacksonville Braves, Hank had a brief but important experience in the Puerto Rican Winter League. Playing winter ball was common for rising stars, providing them with additional experience and exposure. In Puerto Rico, Hank faced diverse competition, further honing his skills and preparing him for the ultimate stage. His time there also exposed him to different styles of play and a broader cultural perspective, enriching his understanding of the game.

Hank's stint with the Jacksonville Braves was brief but pivotal. It was here that he solidified his reputation, showing the Braves' top brass that this young man from Mobile, Alabama, was destined for greatness. His combination of batting prowess, fielding ability, and mental toughness made him stand out to the decision-makers, who recognized they had something special. It wouldn't be long before Hank would be called up to the big leagues.

But let's pause and savor this moment. Before the Major Leagues, before the home runs and the records, there was Hank Aaron—the young man who turned every challenge into an opportunity, every slight into motivation, and every game into a step toward history. His journey through the Negro Leagues and the Minor Leagues wasn't only about stats and awards; it was about character, resilience, and the unyielding pursuit of a dream. Each league, each team, and each season added a layer to Hank's story. The early years with the Clowns showcased his raw talent and adaptability. The seasons with Eau Claire and Jacksonville highlighted his ability to excel under pressure and against adversity. Hank's rise through these ranks was a testament to his extraordinary talent and indomitable spirit. It was a journey marked by significant milestones, each one bringing him closer to the grand stage of Major League Baseball.

Moving on, we step into the grand arena. It was 1954, and the stage was set for Hank Aaron to make his Major League debut with the Milwaukee Braves. Picture the scene: the crowd buzzing with anticipation, the smell of popcorn and hot dogs wafting through the air, and somewhere in the Braves' dugout, a young Hank Aaron putting on his jersey, a mix of nerves and excitement coursing through him.

Hank's journey to the Major Leagues wasn't a straight shot; it was more like a winding road with unexpected turns. But now that he was here, it was time to show everyone what he was made of. He debuted on April 13, 1954, against the Cincinnati Reds. Though he went hitless in his first game, he quickly secured his first Major League hit two days later. The important thing was that Hank was now officially a Major Leaguer.

Despite the slow start, it didn't take long for Hank to find his groove. In his rookie season, he batted .280 with 13 home runs and 69 RBIs. While he did not receive Rookie of the Year honors, his performance laid the foundation for a stellar career that would soon garner league-wide recognition. Not bad for a first-year player finding his footing in the big leagues.

His stats were impressive, but his game style was even more legendary—a quiet confidence and an unflappable demeanor. Hank was the kind of player who let his bat do the talking, and boy, did it have a lot to say. His swing was a thing of beauty—smooth, powerful, and incredibly consistent. Teammates and opponents alike couldn't help but be impressed by his natural talent and work ethic.

The 1955 season was a turning point. Hank upped his game, batting .314 with 27 home runs and 106 RBIs. He made his first All-Star team, a recognition that marked the beginning of a streak that would last for 21 consecutive seasons. Two decades of being recognized as one of the best in the game—not too shabby for a guy who started out hitting bottle caps with a broomstick.

By 1956, Hank was a force to be reckoned with, batting a remarkable .328 and leading the league in hits and total bases. His consistency and ability to deliver in clutch situations made him a nightmare for pitchers. That year also marked his first of four league-leading seasons in total bases, a testament to his power and precision at the plate. But Hank was more than just a power hitter; he was a complete player, contributing with his glove and his speed on the bases as well.

1957 was the year Hank truly arrived. It was a magical season for both him and the Braves. Hank batted .322, hit 44 home runs, and led the league with 132 RBIs. His performance earned him the National League MVP award, a well-deserved recognition of his dominance. But the highlight of the season came on September 23, when Hank hit a game-winning home run to clinch the National League pennant for the Braves. It was a moment of pure elation, not just for Hank, but for the entire city of Milwaukee. The Braves went on to win the World Series, defeating the mighty New York Yankees. Hank batted .393 in the series, proving once again that he was a player for the biggest stages.

The following years saw Hank continue to establish himself as one of the best players in baseball. In 1958, he helped the Braves win another pennant, though they fell short in the World Series. Hank's numbers were consistently stellar, as he regularly hit over .300, belted 30-plus home runs, and drove in over 100 RBIs. His dedication to the game and his team was unwavering. He was not just a star; he was a cornerstone of the Braves' lineup.

As the 1960s began, Hank remained at the peak of his powers. In 1963, he won his second National League home run title with 44 homers, and in 1966, the Braves moved to Atlanta, bringing Hank back to the South. This move was significant for many reasons, not least of which was the opportunity for Hank to play in front of African American fans who idolized him. He embraced his role as a trailblazer, understanding that his success was about more than just personal glory—it was about breaking barriers and inspiring others.

Hank's early years in Atlanta were marked by continued excellence. In 1968, he hit his 500th career home run, joining an elite club of power hitters. He was a model of consistency, rarely missing games and always delivering impressive performances both offensively and defensively. Whether he was hitting for average, power, or playing stellar defense, Hank was the epitome of a complete player.

And let's not forget about Hank's demeanor off the field. Despite his immense success, he remained humble and approachable. He was a family man, devoted to his wife, Barbara, and their children. He understood the importance of giving back to the community, often participating in charity events and speaking out on social issues. Hank's integrity and character were as impressive as his stats, making him a true role model.

As we close this chapter on Hank Aaron's breakthrough and early career, it's clear that his journey was about more than numbers and accolades. It was about overcoming obstacles, breaking barriers, and inspiring generations of players and fans. Hank's story is a testament to what can be achieved with talent, hard work, and an unwavering determination to succeed. And though we won't venture into his later years and legacy here, know that his impact on the game and society continues to resonate, echoing the sound of his powerful swing and the roar of the crowd.

Ted Williams

The Last .400 Hitter

Imagine a kid so obsessed with baseball that he would play in his sleep if he could. That's Theodore Samuel Williams for you, born on August 30, 1918, in sunny San Diego, California. San Diego is known for its beautiful beaches and perfect weather, but young Ted wasn't interested in catching waves; he was more interested in catching fly balls. His father, Samuel Stuart Williams, a World War I veteran, and his mother, May Venzor, who tirelessly worked for the Salvation Army, perhaps never imagined their son would one day be hailed as one of the greatest hitters in baseball history. But hey, everyone starts somewhere, right?

Ted's passion for baseball was like a wildfire—once it sparked, there was no stopping it. Think of a young boy with fierce determination, hitting makeshift baseballs in his backyard, each swing more precise, each throw more accurate. It's like he had baseball coded in his DNA. His first taste of organized baseball came in high school at Herbert Hoover High. He wasn't some underdog story; he was the teenage sensation every pitcher dreaded facing. By the time he graduated in 1936, scouts were already buzzing about this kid who could hit anything thrown his way.

Next up, let's get into the juicy part. At 17, Ted had offers from both the St. Louis Cardinals and the New York Yankees. Yup, those Yankees. But Ted, always the maverick, chose the local San Diego Padres of the Pacific Coast League instead. Why? Because he wanted to stay close to his mom and dad. Cue the collective "aww." But don't be fooled—this wasn't a step down; it was the launchpad of his career. In his rookie season with the Padres, Ted hit .271 with 23 home runs. Not bad for a teenager, huh?

Ted's exploits with the Padres caught the attention of the Boston Red Sox, and in 1937, they purchased his contract. You can almost see the Red Sox scouts high-fiving each other, thinking they struck gold. But they didn't throw him into the deep end right away. Instead, Ted spent some time with the Minneapolis Millers, the Red Sox's minor league team, honing his skills and getting ready for the big leagues. And boy, did he make an impression there. In 1938, he batted .366 with 43 home runs, leading the Millers to the Junior World Series.

Fast forward to 1939, and Ted Williams made his major league debut with the Boston Red Sox. He was no ordinary rookie; he was a phenom who shook the baseball world like an earthquake. Step into Fenway Park and feel the energy—the iconic Green Monster looming in left field—and a 20-year-old kid stepping up to the plate like he owned the place. And, in many ways, he did. In his rookie season, Ted hit .327 with 31 home runs and 145 RBIs. Those numbers are like a cheat code in a video game—simply unreal for a rookie.

Ted's swing was a thing of beauty, a perfect blend of power and precision. It's said he could see the seams on the baseball as it came toward him. Whether that's true or not, his hitting prowess was unquestionable. His left-handed swing, often described as "sweet," was the result of countless hours of practice. Ted would stand in front of a mirror, studying his stance, his swing, his follow-through—making sure everything was perfect. He was like a mad scientist in a lab, always tinkering, always improving.

Ted Williams was all about hitting and had a fiery personality to match—a drive to be the best and an unwavering confidence that sometimes rubbed people the wrong way. He was known for his intense focus and, occasionally, his hot temper. There are stories of him getting into heated arguments with umpires, fans, and even teammates. But that passion, that fire, is what made him so great. He didn't want to be good; he wanted to be the best, and he worked tirelessly to achieve that.

By the end of his first season, Ted had firmly established himself as a force to be reckoned with. He was selected to the All-Star team—a rare feat for a rookie—and finished fourth in the MVP voting. Not too shabby for a kid from San Diego who chose the Padres over the Yankees.

Stepping into the 1940s, Ted Williams was no longer just the rookie sensation; he was transforming into a legend right before everyone's eyes. Fenway Park, with its quirky angles and the Green Monster looming like a mythical beast, was the stage where Ted dazzled the baseball world. The fans, who initially saw him as the promising kid, now revered him as "The Splendid Splinter," a nickname that encapsulated his slender build and superb hitting skills.

In 1941, Ted Williams did something so extraordinary that it still makes baseball fans' jaws drop to this day. He ended the season with a batting average of .406. That's right—over 80 years later, no one has managed to top that. Achieving a batting average over .400 in a sport where a .300 average is considered excellent is quite a feat. Ted walked into the final day of the season with a .3995 average, which would have rounded up to .400 if he had sat out the games. But Ted being Ted, he insisted on playing, going 6-for-8 in a doubleheader against the Philadelphia Athletics and cementing his place in history with a .406 average.

But 1941 had more in store for Ted. That same year, he narrowly missed out on the American League MVP award, finishing second to Joe DiMaggio, who had his own historic 56-game hitting streak. The rivalry between Williams and DiMaggio was the stuff of legends, capturing the imaginations of fans and making every Red Sox-Yankees game a must-watch event.

World War II, however, had different plans for many athletes, and Ted Williams was no exception. In 1942, after another stellar season, he traded his baseball uniform for a military one, enlisting in the Navy and later transferring to the Marine Corps as a fighter pilot—switching the roar of Fenway for the roar of a fighter jet! Ted served valiantly, working as a flight instructor in World War II and flying combat missions during the Korean War, effectively sacrificing nearly five prime years of his baseball career for his country.

When Ted returned to baseball in 1946, he picked up right where he left off. It was like he never missed a beat. He led the Red Sox to the World Series, batting .342 with 38 home runs and 123 RBIs during the regular season, and won his first MVP award. Although the Red Sox lost the Series to the St. Louis Cardinals in seven games, Ted's performance throughout the season reaffirmed his status as one of the game's greatest.

1947 saw Ted achieving another remarkable feat: winning the Triple Crown. He led the league in batting average (.343), home runs (32), and RBIs (114)—a testament to his all-around hitting prowess. Yet, in an almost comical twist of fate, he finished second in the MVP voting again, this time to Joe DiMaggio. It's almost as if the baseball gods enjoyed setting up these dramatic near-misses just to keep things interesting.

The late 1940s and early 1950s were a whirlwind of accolades and records for Ted. In 1949, he won his second MVP award, batting .343 with 43 home runs and 159 RBIs. His ability to hit for both power and average was like finding a unicorn at the end of a rainbow—so rare and so magical. Ted swung for the fences and made the pitchers dance, drawing walks and getting on base. In fact, his career on-base percentage of .482 remains the highest in baseball history.

Ted's dedication to his craft was unparalleled. He was notorious for his intense practice sessions and meticulous attention to detail. He would spend hours in batting practice, refining his swing, studying pitchers, and perfecting his approach. Talking to him about hitting felt like discussing physics with Einstein. He famously said, "I want to walk down the street and have folks say, 'There goes the greatest hitter who ever lived.'" And with every swing, he was inching closer to that dream.

In 1952, after yet another remarkable season, Ted was called back to military duty for the Korean War. Once again, he donned his flight suit and served as a Marine pilot, flying 39 combat missions and earning multiple medals for his bravery. It's almost hard to believe—here was a man who not only mastered the art of hitting a baseball but also flew fighter jets with equal precision and courage. When he returned to the Red Sox in 1953, it was like a superhero coming back to save the day.

Ted's return was nothing short of triumphant. Despite missing so much time, he continued to dominate the league, hitting .407 in 1953, albeit in a shortened season. His ability to perform at such a high level despite the long breaks was astounding. It was like he had a secret stash of baseball magic that he could tap into whenever he picked up a bat.

By the mid-1950s, Ted Williams was an icon. His presence in the lineup made the Red Sox a perennial threat, and his unique persona made him a household name. Kids in Boston and beyond idolized him, mimicking his swing in their backyards, dreaming of one day becoming the next Ted Williams.

By the late 1950s, Ted Williams had already cemented himself as a baseball titan, but he wasn't finished yet. A legend now walked among mortal players, making each at-bat an event. The 1957 season, at the age of 39, Ted once again proved why he was the Splendid Splinter, hitting an astonishing .388. It's almost as if age was nothing but a number to Ted, and he was challenging Father Time to a batting duel—and winning convincingly.

Ted's approach to hitting was still a masterclass in patience and precision. He had this uncanny ability to discern balls from strikes, rarely swinging at bad pitches, which frustrated pitchers to no end. They couldn't trick him; he was like a baseball sorcerer with a bat, anticipating every move. That year, he led the league in on-base percentage and slugging percentage, demonstrating his continued dominance. And let's not forget his .528 on-base percentage that year—the highest ever by a player over 38 years old.

Even as he approached 40, Ted's passion for the game and his competitive spirit showed no signs of waning. The 1958 season saw him hit .328 with 26 home runs, leading the league in walks. Ted was an expert in the art of getting on base, whether by a hit or a walk, always putting pressure on opposing pitchers. His keen eye at the plate was legendary—a product of years of dedication and an almost scientific approach to hitting.

1959, however, brought challenges. Ted was sidelined for much of the season due to injuries, limiting his playtime and effectiveness. It was one of those rare times when the immortal seemed human. He managed to hit .254 in the 75 games he played—a figure that, while respectable for most, was a clear sign that the grueling demands of baseball were catching up with him. But Ted was never one to go down without a fight. His love for the game and his unyielding drive to compete pushed him to return stronger.

In 1960, Ted Williams was determined to finish his career on his terms. His farewell season was a testament to his incredible skill and perseverance. At 42 years old—an age where most players are long retired—Ted hit .316 with 29 home runs. It was as if he were giving one final masterclass in hitting, showing the younger generation how it was done.

The highlight of this season came on September 28, 1960. In his final at-bat, facing the Baltimore Orioles' Jack Fisher, Ted delivered one last moment of magic—a home run. Fenway Park erupted in cheers, fans knowing they were witnessing the end of an era. It was the perfect exclamation point to a storied career—a fitting farewell for the greatest hitter who ever lived.

But let's talk about Ted's relationship with the fans and the media during these final years. Ted was known for his complicated rapport with the press. He often felt they were overly critical and didn't understand his commitment to excellence. This tension occasionally boiled over, resulting in some memorable clashes. However, the fans, despite the occasional friction, adored him. They saw in Ted a relentless pursuit of greatness—a player who wore his heart on his sleeve and gave everything for the game.

Off the field, Ted's later years as a player also highlighted his growing interests outside of baseball. He was an avid fisherman, often seen casting lines in the waters off the Florida coast. His passion for fishing was nearly as strong as his love for baseball, and he often spoke about the tranquility he found on the water, away from the hustle and pressure of the diamond.

Back to the game, though, Ted's influence extended beyond his performance at the plate. Younger players looked up to him, sought his advice, and tried to emulate his work ethic. He became a mentor to many, offering tips and sharing his vast knowledge of hitting. His legacy was not just in the records he set but in the wisdom he imparted to the next generation.

Ted Williams' final season also encapsulated his complex character. He was fiercely independent, often stubborn, but undeniably brilliant. He had an unshakeable belief in his abilities and a drive to excel that never dimmed, even as his career drew to a close. His farewell was a mixture of nostalgia, respect, and awe from fans, players, and even the media that had often been his adversary.

By the end of the 1960 season, Ted Williams had left an indelible mark on the game of baseball. His career stats read like a series of records: a .344 lifetime batting average, 521 home runs, and an on-base percentage of .482. But beyond the numbers, Ted's influence was felt in every corner of the sport. He was the benchmark for hitting excellence—the player against whom all others would be measured.

So, as the 1960 season closed, so did an extraordinary chapter in baseball history. Ted Williams, the kid from San Diego who had captivated the baseball world with his remarkable talent and fiery spirit, had given fans one final season to remember. His farewell home run was more than a hit; it was a statement—a reminder of why he was the Splendid Splinter. And as he walked off the field for the last time, there was no doubt that baseball would never see another like Ted Williams.

Lou Gehrig

The Iron Horse

Let's drop ourselves into a small, sturdy apartment in New York City in the early 1900s. The scent of freshly baked bread wafts through the air, mingling with the distinct aroma of the bustling city streets. In this modest setting, a legend was born—Henry Louis Gehrig, known to the world simply as Lou. But before he stepped onto the iconic baseball diamond, his life was a whirlwind of hard work, family dedication, and unexpected twists that shaped his extraordinary future.

Born on June 19, 1903, Lou was the pride and joy of German immigrants, Heinrich and Christina Gehrig. You might think growing up in the Big Apple would be all about glamorous lights and skyscrapers, but for young Lou, life was more about balancing school with endless chores and dodging his mother's strict, hawk-eyed supervision. Christina, a stern but loving woman, was determined that her son would not follow in the tough footsteps of his father, who worked long, grueling hours as a sheet metal worker. Lou's parents wanted a better life for him, which naturally meant Lou found himself buried in schoolwork and household tasks.

Lou, a sturdy kid with a mop of dark hair and an earnest expression, was lugging heavy baskets of laundry up and down flights of stairs. His arms and legs grew strong from these daily routines, unknowingly preparing him for the powerful swings and speedy sprints that would one day define his baseball prowess. Between his chores, Lou often escaped into the streets for some much-needed respite. And what better way to blow off steam than a quick game of street baseball with the local kids?

Lou's first taste of baseball was far from the professional stadiums and roaring crowds that awaited him. The makeshift baseball fields were the city's parks, and the bases were anything they could find—old cans, crumpled hats, even stacks of newspapers. The bat, often a piece of scrap wood, seemed to transform in his hands as Lou's natural talent began to shine through. Despite the rugged environment, Lou's eyes gleamed with pure joy every time he made contact with the ball. His friends noticed his skill, often choosing him first for their impromptu teams, while Lou remained humble, simply thrilled to be playing.

In school, Lou found himself in scenes straight out of a black-and-white movie: rows of desks, stern teachers, and children scribbling away on chalkboards. Lou was like the middle child of grades—neither top dog nor bottom feeder. His mind wandered frequently to the baseball fields, yet he dutifully completed his assignments, knowing his parents had high hopes for him. Despite the pull of the sport he loved, Lou was determined to respect his parents' wishes and focus on his education.

However, even in school, baseball found its way into Lou's life. His school, PS 132, had a team, and Lou, with his growing reputation on the streets, naturally gravitated towards it. Lou's prowess on the field earned him the admiration of his peers and the notice of his teachers. By the time he reached high school, at Commerce High, Lou's athletic abilities were undeniable. He was like a thunderstorm in the middle of a clear day—sudden, powerful, and impossible to ignore.

During these formative years, Lou encountered one of the pivotal moments of his early life. One day, while playing in a high school game, a scout noticed him. This scout had a knack for spotting hidden gems, and Lou was their crown jewel. The universe was practically high-fiving Lou with every move, every swing, pushing him gently towards his destiny.

Lou's parents, particularly his mother, were still adamant about his academic future. However, the stars were aligning in favor of baseball. His performance caught the attention of Columbia University, which offered him a chance to play while pursuing his studies. To appease his mother, Lou agreed, promising to balance both worlds—the demanding life of a student and the thrilling escapades of a budding athlete.

Lou stepped onto Columbia's fields, feeling the lush grass under his cleats, the smell of freshly cut turf mingling with the cool breeze. It was here that Lou's raw talent began to refine. Under the guidance of coaches who saw his potential, Lou's skills sharpened, his swings grew mightier, and his runs faster. It took no time for him to become the star player, drawing crowds and cheers with every game. In between practices and games, Lou still managed to attend classes, though his mind often drifted to the field. He was living a double life of sorts—a dedicated student by day, a rising baseball star by night. Balancing these worlds wasn't easy, but Lou handled it with a blend of determination and humility that would come to define him throughout his life.

To say his early life was busy would be an understatement. Lou's days were a relentless blend of academics, chores, and baseball, with little room for anything else. Yet, through it all, his love for the game only grew. The joy he found in playing, the camaraderie with teammates, and the thrill of competition all fueled his passion. And with each passing day, it became clearer that Lou Gehrig was destined for greatness—not through a smooth, easy path, but through hard work, dedication, and an unwavering spirit.

By the time he reached his late teens, Lou's journey from the bustling streets of New York to the promising fields of Columbia was paving the way for something even bigger. He had no idea that he was on the brink of stepping into the spotlight of Major League Baseball, where his name would echo through history. But for now, his story was one of a boy with big dreams, navigating the challenges of life with grit and grace, every chore and every swing shaping him into the legend he would become.

The bustling heart of New York City in the 1920s was a whirlwind of jazz, flapper dresses, and the constant hum of progress. This was a time when the city that never sleeps was alive with the energy of the Roaring Twenties. In this vibrant backdrop, Lou Gehrig, having conquered the playgrounds and schoolyards, was about to make a grand entrance onto the biggest stage of all—Major League Baseball.

Fresh out of Columbia University, Lou's transition from college baseball to the big leagues was as swift as one of his powerful swings. Lou was scouted by the New York Yankees, a team that, even then, was beginning to carve out its legendary status. It was 1923 when Lou signed with the Yankees, and it's safe to say, the baseball world was about to be turned on its head.

Lou was there, stepping onto the field at Yankee Stadium for the first time. The sheer enormity of the place, the stands filled with eager fans, and the pressure of wearing the iconic pinstripes would have overwhelmed most. But not Lou. He was as steady as the Rock of Gibraltar. His debut was quiet, almost unassuming, yet every move he made hinted at the greatness that was simmering beneath the surface. Initially, Lou's appearances were sporadic. The Yankees already boasted a strong lineup, and finding a permanent spot was no easy feat. But Lou's talent was undeniable, and it wasn't long before he began to shine. His batting was powerful and consistent, his fielding reliable and robust. Every time he got a chance to play, he made it count.

By 1925, Lou's patience and hard work paid off spectacularly. He was given the opportunity to replace Wally Pipp, the Yankees' regular first baseman, who was out due to a headache. This seemingly minor event turned out to be a pivotal moment in baseball history. Lou seized the opportunity with both hands—literally and figuratively. That day marked the beginning of one of the most extraordinary streaks in sports history: Lou Gehrig would play in 2,130 consecutive games, earning him the nickname "The Iron Horse."

Lou's ascent was less like a rocket launch and more like a mountain climb, powered by pure grit and a rock-solid work ethic. His batting average climbed, his home runs soared, and his RBI count was the stuff of legends. But what truly set Lou apart was his consistency. Day in and day out, he delivered stellar performances, often under immense pressure.

The 1927 Yankees lineup, often referred to as "Murderers' Row," was one of the most formidable in baseball history, and Lou was a key component. With Babe Ruth, the Sultan of Swat, leading the charge, Lou provided the perfect complement. While Ruth dazzled with his flamboyant personality and prodigious home runs, Lou's steadiness provided the backbone the team needed. His batting average for that season was an astonishing .373, with 47 home runs and 175 RBIs, numbers that would be career highlights for most players but were almost routine for Lou.

The camaraderie in the Yankees' locker room was at an all-time high. There was playful banter between teammates, intense strategy discussions, and constant pressure to maintain their dominance. Lou, with his quiet demeanor and relentless work ethic, was a beloved figure among his teammates. His voice was a gentle hum, but his actions were a superhero movie.

By the late 1920s and into the 1930s, Lou Gehrig had firmly established himself as one of baseball's greatest players. His accolades piled up—two MVP awards, multiple All-Star selections, and numerous World Series championships. But beyond the stats, Lou's reputation as a humble, dedicated athlete made him a fan favorite. Kids across America idolized him, mimicking his batting stance and dreaming of one day playing like the Iron Horse.

In the summer of 1934, Lou achieved a milestone that underscored his prowess and consistency. He won the Triple Crown, leading the league in batting average, home runs, and RBIs. This rare feat solidified his status as one of the all-time greats. It was a testament not only to his skill but to his relentless dedication and hard work. Throughout this period, Lou's bond with his parents remained strong. Despite his rising fame and the demands of his career, he always made time for family. He never forgot his roots, often reminiscing about his humble beginnings and the support his parents provided. This grounding influence helped him navigate the challenges and pressures of being a top-tier athlete.

One can only feel the sense of accomplishment and pride Lou must have felt as he looked back on his journey. From the bustling streets of New York to the grandeur of Yankee Stadium, his path was paved with hard work, determination, and an unshakeable love for the game. Every swing of the bat, every run scored, was a testament to his journey—a journey that was far from over but had already etched his name into the annals of baseball history.

As the 1930s progressed, Lou's presence in the Yankees lineup became synonymous with excellence. His streak of consecutive games played continued to build, showcasing not only his skill but his resilience. Through injuries, illnesses, and the wear and tear of countless games, Lou remained steadfast, embodying the spirit of perseverance.

Yet, despite his towering achievements, Lou remained remarkably humble. He often deflected praise, crediting his success to the support of his teammates, the guidance of his coaches, and the unwavering love of his family. This humility, coupled with his undeniable talent, made Lou Gehrig not only a hero on the field but a beloved figure off it. By the late 1930s, we see Lou Gehrig at the peak of his career, a true baseball hero. His journey from a hardworking kid in New York to a shining star in the Major Leagues is nothing short of inspiring. He exemplifies the virtues of hard work, dedication, and humility, qualities that resonate far beyond the baseball diamond.

As the 1930s rolled on, Lou Gehrig stood tall in the annals of baseball greatness. His name was synonymous with power, precision, and resilience. He had become the backbone of the New York Yankees, a team that dominated the Major Leagues with an iron grip. Imagine the atmosphere of Yankee Stadium during those peak years: the crack of the bat, the roar of the crowd, and Lou Gehrig, a towering figure at first base, embodying the spirit of the game.

Lou's peak years were a dazzling display of athletic prowess. His batting average consistently hovered around .340, his home runs and RBIs piling up season after season. The Iron Horse's consecutive games played streak continued to grow, an unbreakable chain of relentless dedication and unyielding performance. Lou's ability to play through pain and adversity was legendary; he was the epitome of toughness in an era that demanded it.

However, life in the big leagues was not without its challenges. The wear and tear of playing every day began to take its toll. Lou experienced his fair share of injuries—sprains, bruises, and strains—that would sideline most players. But not Lou. He powered through with a stoic determination that left fans and fellow players in awe. His secret? A deep-seated love for the game and an unwavering commitment to his team.

By 1936, Lou's reputation as a clutch performer had reached new heights. His ability to deliver in critical moments was almost supernatural. He was the guy you wanted at the plate with the game on the line. His heroics helped lead the Yankees to multiple World Series titles, each victory further solidifying his status as a baseball legend. The 1936 World Series, in particular, showcased Lou's brilliance. Against the formidable New York Giants, Lou's bat was a force of nature, and his leadership on the field was instrumental in the Yankees' triumph.

Amidst the glory, Lou's humility remained a defining trait. While fans and sportswriters showered him with praise, Lou often deflected the accolades to his teammates. He credited the pitchers for their skill, the outfielders for their acrobatics, and his fellow hitters for their contributions. This selflessness endeared him to everyone around him and reinforced the sense of camaraderie that defined the Yankees.

But the late 1930s also brought signs that not all was well. Lou's performance, still remarkable by any standard, began to show subtle signs of decline. His once effortless power seemed a bit strained, his speed around the bases a touch slower. Initially, these changes were attributed to the natural aging process. After all, Lou had been playing at an elite level for over a decade, and even Iron Horses need rest. In 1938, Lou's batting average dipped below .300 for the first time in his career. Though still a force to be reckoned with, the cracks in his armor were becoming more visible. Teammates and fans noticed Lou grimacing more often, his movements less fluid than before. Despite these signs, Lou's spirit remained unbroken. He continued to show up, day after day, embodying the very essence of perseverance.

It was in the 1939 season that the gravity of Lou's situation became impossible to ignore. His once-impeccable coordination seemed to betray him. Routine plays became challenging, and the power in his swings faded. The man who had been an unshakable rock for so long was visibly struggling. Lou, ever the team player, tried to downplay his difficulties, attributing them to minor ailments and fatigue. However, it soon became apparent that something more serious was at play. Lou's performance declined rapidly, and his physical condition worsened. The Yankees, deeply concerned, urged him to seek medical advice. On May 2, 1939, Lou made the heart-wrenching decision to bench himself, ending his legendary consecutive games streak at 2,130. It was a moment that reverberated through the baseball world, marking the end of an era.

On June 19, 1939, Lou Gehrig turned 36. That day, doctors told him he had a illness that would change his life forever. It was really tough news for Lou and his family to hear. But in true Lou Gehrig fashion, he faced it with remarkable courage. Just weeks later, on July 4, 1939, the Yankees organized a special appreciation day in his honor at Yankee Stadium. Standing before a packed crowd, Lou delivered a heartfelt and humble farewell speech. With a voice steady yet filled with emotion, he proclaimed himself 'the luckiest man on the face of the earth.' His words echoed through the stadium, leaving not a single eye dry. In that moment, Lou's grace and dignity shone brighter than ever, solidifying his place as a symbol of resilience and humility

Despite his personal challenges, Lou continued to support his teammates with guidance and encouragement, never losing his love for the game. His courage in the face of illness earned him even greater admiration. Lou's final months were marked by pride in what he had accomplished, leaving behind an unmatched legacy. His famous farewell speech, calling himself 'the luckiest man on the face of the earth,' left a lasting mark on baseball and American culture. As the first player to have his number retired, Lou's story transcends sports, symbolizing strength, humility, and perseverance.

Sandy Koufax

A Left-Handed Legend

Alright, so let's fire up the time machine and go back to the Brooklyn of the early 1940s—a bustling neighborhood where you could smell fresh bagels in the morning and hear the clatter of stickball games in the streets. Amidst this lively scene was a young boy named Sanford Braun, whom you might better know as Sandy Koufax. For young Sandy, the city's heartbeat was his own, and it wouldn't take long before he found himself in the thick of the game.

Sandy came into the world on December 30, 1935, in the borough of Brooklyn, New York. Growing up, he didn't have the luxury of sprawling backyards or open fields. Instead, the concrete jungles and crowded streets became his playgrounds. He lived with his mother, Evelyn, a powerhouse of a woman who balanced work and raising Sandy after separating from his father. Times were tough, but Evelyn's unwavering support provided a strong foundation. Later, when Evelyn remarried, Sandy took the last name of his stepfather, Irving Koufax—a good-natured man who brought much-needed stability to Sandy's life. The change in surname symbolized a new chapter, one filled with hope and opportunity.

In his early years, Sandy was more about basketball than baseball. At Lafayette High School, he was a standout on the hardwood—you'd think he was born to dribble and shoot, slicing through defenses like a hot knife through butter. He loved the thrill of the game, the way the ball felt in his hands, the roar of the crowd after a perfect shot. But fate, with its tricky fingers, had different plans. One day, Sandy's gym teacher, Jack Riley, suggested he give baseball a try as an after-school activity. Sandy hesitated but agreed, maybe thinking it wouldn't hurt to branch out a little.

Now, don't think Sandy picked up a baseball and magically started throwing thunderbolts. His first foray into baseball was more humble. He was a raw talent with a fast arm but as wild as an untrained horse. His pitches could rival a rollercoaster ride—you'd never know where they'd end up. Yet, despite the unpredictability, there was something there—a spark, a glimmer of what could be. Sandy's early days on the diamond were marked by erratic performances and flashes of brilliance. Playing for the Coney Island Sports League and then Lafayette's baseball team, he showed potential that was as wild as it was exciting. It wasn't unusual to see him strike out three batters in a row, then walk the bases loaded. For Sandy, the term "control" was as foreign as ancient hieroglyphics, but he relished the challenge, determined to tame his wild arm.

After high school, Koufax went to the University of Cincinnati on a basketball scholarship—yes, basketball again. Yet, even there, baseball tugged at his sleeve like an insistent child. He couldn't ignore the allure of the diamond. He pitched for the university's baseball team, and his fastball—oh, that fastball—was gaining a reputation. It had the speed of a comet and the unpredictability of a cat on a hot tin roof. Coaches were starting to take notice, and word was spreading like wildfire. Sandy began to realize that maybe his future lay not on the hardwood but on the pitcher's mound.

Here's where things get interesting. In 1954, the Brooklyn Dodgers came calling. Scout Al Campanis had seen enough of Koufax's fiery fastball to convince the Dodgers that this kid was worth a shot, despite his lack of control. So, at the ripe old age of 19, Sandy signed a contract with the Dodgers. But wait, this wasn't your regular contract. No, sir. It was a bonus baby contract, meaning the Dodgers had to keep him on the Major League roster for two years. For Sandy, it was both thrilling and terrifying—talk about trial by fire!

As a 19-year-old, he found himself in the spotlight of Major League Baseball, rubbing shoulders with seasoned pros and legendary players he had only dreamed about. It was overwhelming, to say the least. Koufax's first years with the Dodgers were a mix of awe, struggle, and relentless learning. His fastball was a thing of beauty—when it found the strike zone. More often than not, it was a wild beast, escaping the confines of the plate and sending batters diving for cover. His curveball was another story—a work in progress, as they say. Sandy often grappled with self-doubt, wondering if he truly belonged among the greats.

During these early days, Koufax's teammates saw a young man with immense potential but also immense challenges. He worked tirelessly to hone his skills, spending countless hours with coaches and catching the eye of veterans like Roy Campanella, who saw the diamond in the rough. Campanella's guidance and patience were crucial in those formative years, helping Koufax develop not just his pitches but his confidence.

In these early stages, Sandy Koufax was a study in contrasts. His fastball could light up a radar gun, yet his control issues made every pitch an adventure. Moments of brilliance hinted at the greatness to come; however, inconsistency was his constant companion. But Sandy wasn't one to back down. He faced the ups and downs of a Major League career with grit and determination, resolute in his quest to master his craft.

Let's follow young Sandy as he embarks on the rollercoaster ride of his early Major League career. A gangly kid in a Dodgers uniform stands proudly on the mound at Ebbets Field, the legendary home of the Brooklyn Dodgers. The stadium buzzes with the energy of fans munching hot dogs, kids with wide eyes, and the constant murmur of expectation. For

Sandy, those beginning stages felt like being tossed into the deep end of a pool without knowing how to swim.

From 1955 to 1960, Koufax's time on the mound was a medley of frustrating outings, spectacular flashes of brilliance, and a learning curve that felt more like a steep cliff. The Dodgers, fresh off their 1955 World Series victory, were in the midst of transitioning, and soon they would be relocating to Los Angeles. Amidst these changes, Koufax struggled to find his place. Despite having a fastball that could scorch the air, his lack of control made him a bit of a liability. His ERA (Earned Run Average) often ballooned, making fans and management alike scratch their heads. Here was a pitcher who could strike out anyone on a good day but could also walk half the lineup on a bad one.

Adjusting to life in Los Angeles was another challenge. The familiar streets of Brooklyn were replaced with palm trees and endless sunshine—a stark contrast that left Sandy feeling a bit like a fish out of water. Yet, he remained focused on improving his game. During that time, Sandy was more like a mystery box. He had the potential to be a superstar pitcher but always seemed to miss the mark. His teammates, a mix of grizzled veterans and rising stars, saw him as a project—someone who needed time and patience to harness his natural gifts. His catcher, the wise and experienced Roy Campanella, became his mentor, guiding him through the labyrinth of Major League pitching.

A turning point came in 1959 when Koufax, tired of mediocrity, decided that enough was enough. Frustrated with his lackluster performance, he took a hard look at himself. He began to work on his mechanics, refining his delivery to harness the power of his fastball and the sharp break of his curveball. This was no easy feat. It required countless hours of practice, a relentless work ethic, and an almost stubborn determination to succeed. He studied other pitchers, picking up tips and tricks, and slowly the pieces began to fall into place. For Sandy, it was as much a mental overhaul as a physical one; he started to believe in himself.

The 1960 season was when things started to click. Under the guidance of new pitching coach Joe Becker, Koufax began to show signs of consistency. He progressed bit by bit, and the improvement was noticeable. His strikeout rate climbed, and he started to command his pitches better. Fans and commentators took notice, whispering that maybe, just maybe, Sandy Koufax was beginning to figure it out. Each successful outing bolstered his confidence, and for the first time, Sandy felt like he truly belonged in the Major Leagues.

One of the most memorable games from this period was a match against the arch-rival San Francisco Giants in 1961. The Dodgers-Giants rivalry was one of the fiercest in baseball, adding extra weight to the showdown. Koufax struck out 18 batters, tying the Major League record for strikeouts in a nine-inning game. This was the real deal; it was the payoff from years of grit and hard work. It was as if all the struggles and wild pitches had led to this moment—a showcase of what he was truly capable of. Standing on the mound that day, Sandy felt invincible.

During this time, Koufax's relationship with his teammates deepened. Players like Duke Snider and Don Drysdale saw the transformation firsthand. The kid who had once been a question mark was turning into an exclamation point. Koufax's newfound control and his devastating fastball-curveball combination made him a feared opponent. Batters dreaded facing him, knowing that even if they managed to make contact, the ball would likely end up as a weak grounder or a lazy fly ball.

His climb was boosted by physical changes and a crucial mental shift. Koufax started to understand the game on a deeper level. He learned how to read batters, predict their tendencies, and exploit their weaknesses. With each strikeout, his self-assurance grew. Every triumph boosted his confidence, turning him from a wild rookie pitcher into a master of the mound—a powerhouse who could control the game with exacting precision. For Sandy, the game had transformed from a chaotic struggle into a calculated art form.

The Dodgers, recognizing Koufax's growing prowess, began to rely on him more heavily. He was no longer the rookie with potential; he was a crucial part of their rotation. His performance on the mound translated into more wins for the team and a growing sense of respect from fans and opponents alike. By the early 1960s, as the Dodgers settled into their new home in Los Angeles, Koufax had established himself as a rising star in the Major Leagues. He had overcome the wildness and inconsistency of his initial years through sheer determination and hard work. Each game was a step closer to fulfilling the potential that scouts and coaches had seen in him from the beginning. And while the best was yet to come, these formative years were crucial in shaping the pitcher Sandy Koufax would become.

By the early 1960s, Sandy Koufax was no longer just a promising pitcher finding his footing. He had transformed into a veritable titan on the mound. The years of refining his technique, building his confidence, and understanding the intricacies of pitching had all come together to forge a weapon that could dominate even the most fearsome of hitters. The Dodgers knew they had something special. The rest of the league was about to find out just how special.

1961 and 1962 were critical years, but it was the 1963 season that marked Koufax's emergence as an unstoppable force. During this season, Sandy put together one of the most dominant pitching performances in baseball history. He finished the year with a 25-5 record, an ERA of 1.88, and a mind-boggling 306 strikeouts. It was as if he had finally unlocked the secret to pitching immortality. Standing on the mound, Sandy felt an exhilarating sense of control and mastery. Batters across the league dreaded facing him, and fans flocked to the stadium to witness his artistry.

The 1963 World Series showcased Koufax at his peak. Facing the storied New York Yankees under the bright lights of the World Series, Sandy felt the weight of the moment but also an inner calm. He knew he was ready. In Game 1, he struck out 15 batters, setting a World Series record and leading the Dodgers to a 5-2 victory. The roar of the crowd was deafening, but inside, he was focused, serene. He returned in Game 4 to pitch a complete game shutout, securing the championship for the Dodgers. Koufax's ability to rise to the occasion on the biggest stage solidified his reputation as one of the game's greats.

But it was far from a walk in the park. Behind the scenes, Koufax was fighting arthritis in his left elbow, a condition that brought him heaps of pain and put his career on the line. Every pitch sent a jolt of agony through his arm. The fact that he could perform at such a high level while dealing with this chronic pain was a testament to his toughness and determination. Nights were sleepless, and days were filled with treatments, but he refused to let the pain define him. He often pitched through pain that would sideline lesser players, driven by an unyielding desire to compete and win.

The 1965 season brought more brilliance and more challenges. Koufax achieved another milestone by pitching a perfect game against the Chicago Cubs on September 9, 1965. This was no ordinary perfect game; it was a dazzling display of precision and power. Standing on the mound during that perfect game, every pitch felt right. It was as if time slowed down, and Sandy was in complete harmony with the game. He struck out

14 batters and allowed no one to reach base, cementing his place in baseball lore. That same year, he won his second Cy Young Award and led the Dodgers to another World Series title, pitching a shutout in Game 7 against the Minnesota Twins on two days' rest. Exhausted but determined, he summoned every ounce of strength to deliver when it mattered most. Two days! Talk about superhuman.

Yet, the relentless pain in his elbow grew worse, and Koufax's pre-game routine became increasingly grueling. He would immerse his arm in ice baths, take painkillers, and undergo treatments that were more akin to torture than therapy. There were days he questioned how much longer he could endure it. But despite the agony, he continued to dominate, driven by an unquenchable competitive fire and a love for the game that overshadowed the pain.

1966 was another stellar year, marked by a third Cy Young Award and a third ERA title. Koufax finished the season with a 27-9 record and an ERA of 1.73. His strikeouts that year totaled 317, further solidifying his status as a strikeout king. Yet, each victory was bittersweet. The pain had reached a tipping point, and Sandy knew he was at a crossroads. The offseason was spent in deep contemplation, wrestling with the heartbreaking realization that continuing to pitch could cause permanent damage to his arm.

Throughout these peak years, Koufax's influence extended beyond the mound. He was a quiet leader in the clubhouse, respected by teammates for his work ethic, humility, and sheer talent. Players like Don Drysdale and Maury Wills looked up to him not just for his performance but for his perseverance and the way he handled the pressures of fame and expectation. In an era when the spotlight could easily inflate egos, Sandy remained grounded, setting an example for players across the league.

As the 1966 season ended, the toll of constant pain and the rigorous demands of pitching made it clear that Koufax had to make a decision about his future. It was a painful realization, but one he faced with the same courage he showed on the mound. Though the baseball world hoped for many more years of his brilliance, Sandy Koufax's time on the mound was drawing to a close. His body had given all it could. With a heavy heart but a sense of gratitude, he stepped away from the game he loved, his legacy as one of the greatest pitchers ever firmly established.

Roberto Clemente

The Great One

Okay boys, I'm about to take you on a wild ride through the amazing life of Roberto Clemente. We're on a sun-drenched island, with the sound of waves crashing on the shore and the smell of delicious food in the air. The location is Carolina, Puerto Rico, and it's August 18, 1934. That's right, we're going back in time to the day Roberto Clemente came into this world. Little did anyone know, this baby boy would grow up to be one of the greatest baseball players ever, with a heart as big as his batting average.

Roberto was born into a large family, the youngest of seven children. His father, Melchor Clemente, worked as a foreman in the sugarcane fields, which sounds sweet but was actually tough work. His mother, Luisa, managed the household, which was like being the CEO of a small company, only with more cooking and fewer board meetings. From a young age, Roberto was all about helping his family. He carried milk for a dairy, sold vegetables, and did anything he could to pitch in. But amid all that hard work, he had a passion that was beginning to grow like wildfire—baseball.

Young Roberto, around the age of eight, was a guy with a makeshift bat and a ball that was probably more tape than leather. He and his friends played in empty lots, making up for their lack of proper equipment with an abundance of enthusiasm and creativity. The crack of the bat, the cheers of his friends—this was Roberto's playground, and he was quickly becoming the star.

As he grew older, his talent became impossible to ignore. By the time he was in high school, he was already a standout. Roberto attended Julio Vizcarrondo Coronado High School, where he excelled in track and field too. That's right—he could run fast, throw far, and hit hard. He was like a superhero in a baseball uniform. Imagine being able to run like The Flash and throw a ball like a cannon—that's how Roberto was. His athletic abilities were astonishing, and it was clear he was destined for greatness.

In 1952, at the age of 18, Roberto started playing for the Santurce Cangrejeros in the Puerto Rican Winter League. This wasn't some casual weekend league; it was packed with serious talent, including future Major League Baseball (MLB) stars. Roberto's performance there was like a fireworks display on the Fourth of July—impossible to ignore. He batted .288 that season, but more importantly, his skills caught the eyes of MLB scouts.

Here's where things start to get really exciting. The Brooklyn Dodgers took notice of Roberto and signed him to a minor league deal. This was a huge deal—the Dodgers were one of the premier teams in baseball, and their interest in Roberto showed just how special he was. But there's a twist in our tale. The Dodgers tried to hide Roberto by sending him to play for their minor league team, the Montreal Royals, hoping other teams wouldn't notice his talent. Spoiler alert: it didn't work.

In 1954, the Pittsburgh Pirates swooped in and selected Roberto in the Rule 5 Draft, which basically meant they saw him and said, "We need that guy on our team, right now."

Roberto was off to the big leagues. A young guy travels to a foreign land, and pow, he's playing in the big leagues—it was like jumping straight into the deep end of the pool without a floatie.

Roberto made his major league debut on April 17, 1955, at the age of 20. It was a challenging start; he struggled with injuries and adapting to a new environment. But here's the thing about Roberto: he didn't give up. He had a warrior spirit, fueled by the dreams of a kid playing baseball with his friends back in Puerto Rico. His first season was a mix of highs and lows, but everyone could see the flashes of brilliance that hinted at his future greatness.

Throughout these early years, Roberto's personality shone through. He was determined, hardworking, and full of quiet confidence. He wasn't flashy off the field, but when he played—oh boy—it was like poetry in motion. He had an arm that could throw runners out from deep in the outfield and a bat that could send baseballs soaring into the stands. His teammates and fans quickly learned that Roberto Clemente was something special. And so, we leave Roberto at the beginning of his MLB journey, poised for the incredible career that lay ahead. He had come a long way from the dusty fields of Carolina, Puerto Rico, but his journey was just beginning. Stay tuned for the next segment, where we'll follow Roberto as he cements his place among baseball's elite, turning his natural talent into a force that would change the game forever.

So, there Roberto Clemente was, stepping into the spotlight of Major League Baseball with the Pittsburgh Pirates. He experienced the crack of the bat, the roar of the crowd, and the smell of hot dogs wafting through the stands. But his start was like a ship battling rough seas. The mid-1950s in America was a time of big changes and even bigger challenges, especially for a young player from Puerto Rico.

Roberto faced a language barrier as daunting as a 100-mph fastball. English was not his first language, and navigating interviews, team meetings, and daily life in the United States required a crash course in communication. But Roberto was nothing if not determined. He worked tirelessly to learn English, often practicing with teammates, studying on his own, and immersing himself in the language. His perseverance paid off, but it didn't stop people from misinterpreting his words and intentions. Reporters often misquoted him, which led to some frustrating and unfair headlines. Yet, he handled it with grace, focusing on his game and letting his performance do the talking.

Speaking of performance, let's talk about the 1960 World Series. By this time, Roberto had firmly established himself as a key player for the Pirates. The World Series that year was a nail-biter against the New York Yankees. Let's feel the tension—each game a battle, each inning a test of nerves. The series stretched to seven games, with the final showdown held at Forbes Field. It was during this game that Bill Mazeroski hit the legendary walk-off home run, clinching the championship for the Pirates. While Mazeroski's homer stole the headlines, Roberto's contributions throughout the series were indispensable. He batted .310 and was a rock in the outfield, showcasing his incredible arm and defensive skills.

Roberto's performance in the 1960s was a testament to his dedication and talent. Year after year, he dazzled fans and confounded pitchers. In 1961, he achieved a batting average of .351, which was the highest in the National League. Trying to hit a tiny baseball coming at you at lightning speed, and then doing it consistently better than almost anyone else—that's what Roberto did. His secret? Relentless practice, a keen eye, and a deep understanding of the game. He knew the pitchers, understood their strategies, and could predict where the ball would be, almost like he had a sixth sense.

Roberto's batting was stellar, but his all-around play turned him into a baseball legend. He won his first Gold Glove Award in 1961, an honor given to the best defensive players. Then he won it again in 1962, 1963, and so on, until he had a total of 12 Gold Gloves. Bagging the top spot twelve times—that's major boss vibes! Roberto's throws from right field were like laser-guided missiles, accurately nailing runners trying to stretch singles into doubles. His speed, agility, and pinpoint accuracy made him a highlight reel unto himself.

Despite his on-field success, Roberto faced numerous challenges. As a Latin American player in the 1960s, he encountered prejudice and discrimination. It wasn't uncommon for him to hear derogatory comments from fans and even some players. Instead of letting it bring him down, Roberto used it as fuel for his fire. He remained proud of his heritage and worked to bridge the gap between different cultures, speaking out against injustice and fighting for the respect he knew all players deserved. His courage in addressing these issues was as remarkable as his athletic prowess.

Roberto's dedication extended beyond the baseball diamond. He was deeply committed to humanitarian efforts, often returning to Puerto Rico in the off-season to help his community. He believed in using his platform to make a difference, a sentiment that resonated with his fans and fellow players. His generosity and compassion earned him immense respect and admiration, both on and off the field.

The 1966 season marked a major milestone in Roberto Clemente's legendary career. He batted .317, but it was his all-around brilliance that stood out. His cannon arm and pinpoint accuracy in the outfield made him one of the most feared defenders in baseball. Clemente's relentless and consistent play elevated his reputation across the league, and his MVP award was a fitting tribute to a season where everything clicked. Each swing of the bat seemed to send the ball soaring, and every throw from right field was a masterpiece. It was a year of precision, power, and his unyielding pursuit of greatness, cementing him as a fan favorite and a nightmare for opposing teams.

In 1967, Clemente further reinforced his status among baseball's elite. While he didn't capture another MVP, his performance remained stellar. He continued to showcase the same power, precision, and poise that had defined his MVP season, making every play look effortless and further building on his legacy of athletic brilliance.

But even superheroes have their battles. Roberto struggled with chronic back pain, a result of years of pushing his body to the limit. Despite the pain, he rarely let it show, playing through discomfort and continuing to perform at an elite level. His resilience and determination were truly awe-inspiring, and his ability to persevere through adversity endeared him even more to his fans.

As the 1960s drew to a close, Roberto Clemente was at the peak of his career—a symbol of excellence, resilience, and integrity. He had become more than a baseball player; he was a beacon of hope and a role model for aspiring athletes everywhere. His journey from the streets of Carolina, Puerto Rico, to the pinnacle of Major League Baseball was a testament to what hard work, talent, and unwavering determination could achieve.

And here we are, on the edge of our seats, ready to explore the climax of Roberto Clemente's illustrious career. By the late 1960s and early 1970s, Roberto was a titan of the game, a player who had transformed raw talent and relentless effort into a legacy of greatness. He was giving baseball a brand-new style.

Let's rewind to the 1971 World Series, a spectacular showcase of Roberto's skills. The Pirates were up against the Baltimore Orioles, a team brimming with talent. The series was a rollercoaster of emotions, with the Pirates fighting tooth and nail in each game. Roberto shone brighter than ever, hitting safely in all seven games, finishing with a dazzling .414 batting average. He hit two home runs during the series, including one in the decisive Game 7. His performance was so remarkable that he was named the World Series MVP. Imagine the thrill of watching your hero dominate on the biggest stage, delivering clutch hits and making jaw-dropping plays in the field. That was Roberto Clemente, making the impossible seem effortless.

Roberto's talent shone bright in all corners, beyond the World Series. Throughout the early 1970s, he continued to rack up accolades and break records. In 1972, he achieved a monumental milestone: his 3,000th hit. The packed Three Rivers Stadium came alive with the buzzing crowd. On September 30, 1972, Roberto stepped up to the plate and delivered a crisp, line-drive double off Jon Matlack of the New York Mets. The stadium erupted in cheers as Roberto stood on second base, tipping his cap to the adoring fans. This hit placed him in the exclusive club of players with 3,000 career hits, a testament to his consistent brilliance at the plate.

But Roberto's impact wasn't measured in hits alone. His defensive prowess was legendary. Opposing runners feared challenging his arm, knowing that attempting to take an extra base could end in an embarrassing out. His throws were laser-precise, and his ability to cover ground in the outfield was unmatched. He played the game with a grace and fluidity that left fans and fellow players in awe. It was as if he had a personal agreement with the baseball gods, allowing him to make plays others could only dream of.

Roberto's commitment to excellence extended beyond his physical abilities. He was a student of the game, constantly analyzing pitchers, refining his batting technique, and studying opponents. His preparation was meticulous, his focus unwavering. This dedication earned him the respect of his peers and the admiration of fans. He loved being good, but being the best was his ultimate goal, so he soared higher every season.

Throughout his career, Roberto remained a beacon of integrity and sportsmanship. He approached every game with a fierce competitive spirit but never lost sight of the importance of respect and humility. His interactions with fans were heartfelt, his conduct on the field exemplary. He played for the love of the game and the joy of competition, inspiring countless young athletes to pursue their dreams with the same passion and dedication.

Off the field, Roberto continued his humanitarian work, using his fame and resources to make a difference in the lives of others. He organized baseball clinics for underprivileged children, both in Puerto Rico and the United States, sharing his knowledge and love of the game. His generosity and commitment to community service were integral parts of who he was. He believed in giving back, in lifting others up, and in using his success to bring positive change.

Roberto Clemente's career was a tapestry of remarkable achievements and unforgettable moments. He played with a heart full of passion, a spirit unyielding in the face of challenges, and a determination that propelled him to the pinnacle of the sport. He was a true artist on the baseball diamond, crafting a legacy that would endure for generations.

As we conclude, we leave him at the height of his powers—a symbol of excellence and perseverance. His story is a testament to the power of hard work, the importance of character, and the impact one person can have on the world. So next time you pick up a bat, throw a ball, or simply dream of greatness, remember Roberto Clemente—the kid from Carolina who became a legend.

Mickey Mantle

The Oklahoma Kid

Alright, so let's put ourselves somewhere in Commerce, Oklahoma, a place that's so small, you might miss it if you blink twice. This tiny town is where Mickey Mantle, the kid who would one day be known as "The Commerce Comet," started his legendary journey. Born on October 20, 1931, Mickey's childhood was the stuff of classic Americana – think pick-up games of baseball in dusty fields, wild adventures, and a family that knew a thing or two about the sport. His dad, Elvin Charles Mantle, known as "Mutt," had baseball running through his veins and passed that passion down to his son. You see, Mutt was determined to make sure Mickey knew how to swing a bat before he could even walk.

Mutt and Mickey were in the backyard, the summer sun blazing down and the smell of freshly cut grass in the air. Little Mickey, no taller than a corn stalk, was gripping a bat that seemed almost as big as he was. Mickey learned to switch-hit from an early age. Mutt would pitch left-handed and right-handed to ensure Mickey could handle anything thrown his way. The goal was simple: make Mickey the most versatile hitter around. And boy, did that plan work out!

But let's not speed ahead too fast. Mickey's early life was more than batting and blue skies. He was also a standout in football and basketball at Commerce High School, a triple-threat athlete before the term was even cool. Yet, despite his prowess on the football field and the basketball court, baseball was his true love. This was crystal clear when in his sophomore year, Mickey was struck in the shin by a football cleat, developing osteomyelitis, a disease that almost led to his leg being amputated. Can you think of a world without Mickey Mantle because of one bad hit on the football field? Fortunately, his quick-thinking parents got him to the hospital in time, and with the help of the then-newly discovered penicillin, Mickey's leg was saved. A close call, right?

Fast forward to Mickey's senior year. The Yankees' scout Tom Greenwade happened to catch one of Mickey's games, and let's just say he was more than impressed. The ball seemed to fly off Mickey's bat as if it had a mind of its own, eager to make a grand exit over the fences. Greenwade saw potential – no, scratch that – he saw a future legend. Signing Mickey to a minor league contract in 1949 for $140 a week (a princely sum for a teenager back then) was a no-brainer.

Now young Mickey, fresh out of Commerce, is heading to Independence, Kansas, to play for the Independence Yankees, a Class D minor league team. It was here that Mickey's raw talent began to turn heads. The kid had power, speed, and a natural instinct for the game. However, life in the minors was part baseball, part survival course. The road trips were long, the motels were questionable, and the pay – well, let's just say Mickey wasn't exactly living in luxury. But none of that mattered when he stepped onto the field.

Here's a quirky tidbit: Mickey's first professional season had more bumps than a dirt road. Sure, he showed flashes of brilliance, but he also struggled, especially with striking out. However, those who watched him play saw the spark – that undeniable talent that hinted at future greatness. And that spark caught fire in 1950 when he moved up to the Class C Joplin Miners. Mickey batted an astonishing .383 with 26 home runs. People started to take serious notice.

The defining moment came during the Yankees' spring training in 1951. Mickey, the young phenom from Oklahoma, was rubbing shoulders with the legends – Joe DiMaggio, Yogi Berra, and Phil Rizzuto. It was like walking into a superhero convention, and Mickey was the new kid on the block. Despite his nerves, Mickey impressed everyone with his bat speed and power, even earning the nickname "Muscles" from his teammates. But it wasn't a smooth ride – he got off to a rocky start, got sent down to the minors, and almost quit baseball altogether. Luckily, a pep talk from his father and a call back to the majors reignited his determination.

So, imagine it's a crisp April day in 1951, and Mickey Mantle steps onto the field for his major league debut. The crowd at Yankee Stadium buzzes with excitement, unaware they are witnessing the start of something extraordinary. Number 6 (yes, he wore 6 before he got his famous number 7) took the field with the confidence of a seasoned pro and the heart of a kid living his dream. The rest, as they say, is history – but let's save that for later.

Fast forward to Mickey Mantle's breakout season. Yankee Stadium in the 1950s – a coliseum of baseball dreams, packed with fans, the scent of hot dogs and popcorn wafting through the air, the clamor of excited chatter filling the stands. Mickey Mantle had arrived, and the baseball world was buzzing. Here was a guy who could hit the ball so far it looked like it was going to orbit the Earth. His switch-hitting prowess was becoming legendary, making pitchers quake in their cleats. But with great power comes great responsibility – and a fair share of struggles.

Mickey's 1956 season was the stuff of legend. This was the year he won the Triple Crown, leading the league in batting average (.353), home runs (52), and RBIs (130). It was as if

Mickey was in a league of his own, a superhero among mere mortals. Fans packed the stadiums to see him play, and sportswriters couldn't get enough of him. They hailed him as the new face of baseball, the guy who would carry the Yankees' torch into the future.

But let's pause here and sprinkle in some humor, because Mickey wasn't without his quirks. Take his diet, for example. Despite being an elite athlete, Mickey was notorious for his less-than-ideal eating habits. He was known to down multiple hot dogs and drink copious amounts of soda – sometimes right before a game! What if a modern-day player did that – Twitter would explode! Yet, somehow, it worked for Mickey. He'd munch on a couple of hot dogs, step up to the plate, and whack the ball out of the park. Go figure!

Mickey's career had big swings and bigger misses. He faced his fair share of obstacles, too. Injuries seemed to follow him like a shadow, starting with that infamous knee injury in the 1951 World Series. Chasing a fly ball, he tangled with a drain cover in the outfield, tearing his knee up. Despite this, Mickey played through the pain, embodying the true spirit of a ballplayer. Think of trying to play baseball – let alone at the highest level – with a bum knee. Ouch, right?

The 1957 and 1958 seasons saw Mickey continue to dominate the league, though the injuries persisted. He was a constant presence at the All-Star games, a fixture in the MVP races, and an icon of American sports. But beneath the surface, the injuries were taking their toll. Mickey's knees were often wrapped in ice, and he played through pain that would sideline most players. His perseverance was heroic, like a knight battling dragons with a dull sword.

And then there were the slumps. Even legends have off days, and Mickey was no exception. Step up to the plate with the weight of a city's expectations on your shoulders, and feel the pressure of swinging and missing repeatedly. During one particularly brutal slump, Mickey famously took to practicing with a bat in one hand, trying to recalibrate his swing. Talk about dedication! He'd spend hours in the batting cage, sweat pouring down his face, determined to get back to form. It's a testament to his grit that he always found his way out of those slumps, often coming back stronger.

Off the field, Mickey's life was a whirlwind. He became a celebrity, his every move tracked by adoring fans and relentless reporters. But Mickey remained a small-town boy at heart, often uncomfortable with the spotlight. He preferred hanging out with his teammates, sharing laughs and stories, rather than hobnobbing with the elite. And let's not forget his legendary sense of humor – Mickey loved a good prank, whether it was filling a teammate's locker with shaving cream or convincing rookies of ridiculous superstitions. Imagine being the new guy, taking Mickey's advice seriously, and hopping on one foot before at-bats because you thought it brought good luck!

Despite the fun and games, the pressure was immense. Mickey was expected to fill the shoes of Joe DiMaggio, and that's no small task. The fans, the media, the team – everyone looked to Mickey to lead the Yankees to victory. And lead he did, with a bat that seemed to channel the thunder and legs that – when healthy – were as fast as lightning. But the weight of those expectations could be crushing. Mickey often spoke about the fear of failure, about not living up to the hype. Yet, he faced those fears head-on, every time he stepped onto the diamond.

One of Mickey's most iconic moments came during the 1961 season, the year of the great home run race between him and Roger Maris. Picture it: Two Yankees teammates, both gunning for Babe Ruth's single-season home run record of 60. The media turned it into a gladiatorial contest, but Mickey and Roger remained close friends throughout. Mickey hit 54 home runs that season, a staggering number that would have broken the record in any other year. Unfortunately, his campaign was cut short by a severe hip infection, leading to a trip to the hospital and sidelining him for the final stretch. Roger Maris ultimately broke the record with 61 home runs, but Mickey's effort that year is still remembered as one of the greatest displays of power hitting.

Injuries continued to plague Mickey in the following years, but he never stopped being a force at the plate. His ability to switch-hit with power was unrivaled, and he continued to rack up accolades and All-Star appearances. Despite the physical toll, Mickey's love for the game never waned. He played with the enthusiasm of a kid from Commerce, Oklahoma, every single day.

As we journey further into Mickey Mantle's career, we find a player who, despite the physical toll on his body, continued to showcase resilience and raw talent. The 1960s were a time of triumph and turbulence for Mickey. Even as injuries chipped away at his once-unstoppable form, he remained a formidable presence on the field, a testament to his sheer willpower and dedication to the game.

In the early '60s, Mickey's performances still dazzled the crowds. One of the most memorable moments came on June 5, 1963, during a game against the Kansas City Athletics. Mantle crushed a pitch so hard it rocketed over the right-center field bleachers at Yankee Stadium, a jaw-dropping 500 feet away. The ball actually struck the façade of the stadium's upper deck, narrowly missing becoming the first fair ball to leave Yankee Stadium entirely. It's one of those moments where you wish you could have seen the faces of the fans and the pitcher – pure astonishment.

But life wasn't all home runs and standing ovations. Injuries, the uninvited guests that they were, continued to haunt Mickey. His knees were particularly troublesome, often swollen and painful, requiring constant care and attention. There were days when just walking was a challenge, yet Mickey would still put on his uniform and give his all. It's like having a favorite toy that's worn out but you keep playing with it because of all the memories and joy it brings – that's how Mickey felt about baseball.

Then there were the turbulent times, moments that tested Mickey's spirit and resolve. Off the field, Mickey struggled with personal issues, which sometimes spilled into his professional life. The expectations, the pressure, the physical pain – it all took a toll. But through it all, Mickey remained an icon, beloved by fans and respected by peers. His ability to persevere through adversity only added to his legend. Facing a fastball from Sandy Koufax while battling your own personal demons is like a superhero fighting villains both outside and within.

One of the most touching aspects of Mickey's later career was his role as a mentor to younger players. Despite his struggles, he always took time to share his knowledge and experience. Mickey's playful nature made him a favorite in the clubhouse, but he also knew when to be serious and impart wisdom. It's like having a big brother who's both fun and wise, guiding you through the rough patches with a mix of humor and insight.

In 1964, the Yankees reached the World Series again, facing off against the St. Louis Cardinals. Mickey had an outstanding series, belting three home runs, including a walk-off shot in Game 3. It was classic Mickey – stepping up in the big moments and delivering when it mattered most. The series went to seven games, and although the Yankees ultimately fell short, Mickey's performance was a highlight, a reminder of his enduring talent and clutch capability.

However, the Yankees' dominance began to wane in the mid-60s, and with it, Mickey's physical capabilities continued to decline. The team that had been a perennial power-house started to struggle, marking the end of an era. Mickey, though still a significant player, began to feel the wear and tear more acutely. By **1967**, he shifted from center field to first base in an attempt to lessen the strain on his legs. It was a bittersweet transition, like seeing your favorite superhero hang up their cape and take on a less demanding role.

In 1968, Mickey Mantle hit his 536th and final home run, solidifying his place in the annals of baseball history. This home run moved him past the great Jimmie Foxx into third place on the all-time home run list at that time. Fans everywhere knew they were witnessing the final chapters of an extraordinary career. Mickey's body might have been faltering, but his spirit was unbreakable. Every time he stepped up to the plate, there was a chance for magic – a flash of the brilliance that had defined his career.

The final game of Mickey Mantle's career came on September 28, 1968. The stadium was packed, fans eager to see their hero one last time. As he took his final swings, the crowd roared, an outpouring of love and respect for a player who had given them so much joy. When he tipped his cap and walked off the field, it marked the end of an era – an era defined by breathtaking home runs, incredible resilience, and an unwavering love for the game.

Mickey Mantle's career was a rollercoaster of epic proportions, filled with soaring highs and gut-wrenching lows. Yet through it all, Mickey remained the quintessential ballplayer, embodying the spirit of baseball with every swing of his bat. He was a hero, a mentor, and a legend – the kind of player who comes along once in a lifetime. And while his later years might have been marked by turbulence, the triumphs he achieved ensured that his legacy would endure for generations to come.

Amazing Facts, Legends, and Moments

Pitchers Who Made History

Nolan Ryan's Thunderbolt Arm: Nolan Ryan, a human lightning bolt, hurls the fastest pitches the game has ever seen. With a fastball clocking in at an eye-watering 108 mph, Ryan's arm was like a cannon. This Texan titan served up 5,714 strikeouts, more than anyone in MLB history. Ryan's career showcased incredible endurance, allowing him to pitch an unbelievable 27 years in the majors, during which he crafted seven no-hitters - a record that remains unbroken to this day.

Sandy Koufax's Perfect Art: Sandy Koufax, known as "The Left Arm of God," turned pitching into poetry. Though cut short by injury, his career shone brightly with moments like his perfect game in 1965, one of just 23 perfect games in MLB history. Koufax struck out 14 batters in that game, making art from every pitch. Over four seasons from 1963 to 1966, he dominated with an ERA (earned run average) that seemed to defy gravity, leading the league each year and cementing his legacy in the golden era of baseball.

Bob Gibson's Intimidating Aura: Bob Gibson, with a glare that could freeze batters in their tracks, was the embodiment of intimidation. In 1968, Gibson posted a 1.12 ERA, a number so staggeringly low that MLB lowered the pitching mound the following year to give batters a fighting chance. Gibson's dominance in the World Series was unmatched, racking up eight games and striking out 92 batters across nine appearances.

Randy Johnson's Bird Strike: If you see a 6'10" giant on the mound - that's Randy Johnson, also known as "The Big Unit." Famous for his fastball and devastating slider, Johnson also became an unwilling viral sensation when, during a 2001 spring training game, one of his pitches collided with a bird in mid-air. The event, a rare and shocking moment, underscored the sheer speed of his pitches. With 4,875 strikeouts, Johnson's career is a testament to the power and precision of a man who was literally and figuratively a giant in the game.

Pedro Martinez's Pitching Precision: Pedro Martinez, a magician on the mound, had an arsenal of pitches that seemed to bend reality. At the height of the steroid era, Martinez posted an ERA of 1.74 in 2000, a feat akin to defying overwhelming odds and emerging victorious. His 3,154 career strikeouts tell the story of a pitcher who outsmarted batters, making each pitch a battle of wits.

Mariano Rivera's Cutter: Enter Sandman, Mariano Rivera, the closer who brought games to a serene end with just one pitch: the cutter. This pitch, thrown with the precision of a master craftsman, shattered bats and dreams alike, earning Rivera 652 saves, the most in MLB history. His postseason ERA of 0.70 over 141 innings is the stuff of legend, a testament to his calm under pressure.

Roger Clemens' Rocket Fuel: Roger Clemens, known as "The Rocket," had a career that soared as high as his nickname suggests. With 4,672 strikeouts and 354 wins, Clemens' dominance on the mound was powered by a fastball that seemed to defy time, remaining potent across three decades of baseball. His seven Cy Young Awards, given to the best pitchers, are a trophy case for his excellence and longevity.

Cy Young's Everlasting Record: Speaking of Cy Young Awards, let's talk about the man himself, Cy Young. With a career that spanned 22 seasons, Young's record of 511 wins is a peak so high that no pitcher has ever come close since. This titan of the early days of baseball set standards that today's pitchers still dream of reaching.

Greg Maddux's Surgical Precision: Greg Maddux, "The Professor," pitched not with overwhelming power but with surgical precision. His ability to place a pitch exactly where he wanted allowed him to outthink and outplay batters, leading to four consecutive Cy Young Awards from 1992 to 1995. Maddux's 355 career wins and 3.16 ERA over 23 seasons are a testament to the power of the mind in the game of baseball.

Satchel Paige's Ageless Wonder: Lastly, Satchel Paige, the ageless wonder of baseball, didn't make his MLB debut until he was 42 due to the color barrier. Yet, he dazzled fans and baffled hitters well into his 50s (and, by some accounts, his 60s) with a pitching style that was as flamboyant as it was effective. His career, spanning multiple decades and leagues, is a story of perseverance, talent, and an unyielding love for the game.

Food Curiosities

The Colossal Nacho Platter: A nacho platter so vast that it stretches longer than a baseball diamond's baseline... That's exactly what the University of Kansas fans witnessed in April 2012. This gargantuan snack weighed a staggering 4,689 pounds, earning its place in the Guinness World Records. Loaded with nacho cheese, meat, jalapeños, and more, it wasn't just a sight to behold but a communal feast that brought fans together in a shared, cheesy delight.

Cracker Jack's Birth: A staple at baseball games, Cracker Jack's inception is as American as the sport itself. Introduced in 1896, this blend of caramel-coated popcorn and peanuts became synonymous with baseball after being immortalized in the 1908 song "Take Me Out to the Ball Game." The creation by Frederick and Louis Rueckheim marked a pivotal moment in snack history, marrying sweet and savory flavors in a box filled with surprises, including a prize in every pack, which made it a hit among kids and adults alike.

The $80 Hot Dog: In 2011, the Brockton Rox, a team known for its culinary creativity, unveiled the "K-O Dog," a luxurious snack priced at $80, setting a record for the world's most expensive hot dog at the time. It was a half-pound all-beef foot-long hot dog, deep-fried and coated in truffle oil, dusted with porcini mushrooms, and topped with white truffle shavings, crème fraiche, caviar, and fresh roe, all served in a blini roll. This gourmet twist on a classic blended the worlds of fine dining and casual sports viewing in one unforgettable bite, showcasing the team's innovative approach to ballpark cuisine.

Giant Glove Grub: At AT&T Park (now Oracle Park), home of the San Francisco Giants, fans can enjoy a dish served in a 22-inch replica of a baseball glove. Dubbed the "Glove Bowl," it's a novelty and a culinary challenge. Filled with nachos, this enormous serving is meant for sharing, embodying the spirit of teamwork and camaraderie at the heart of baseball. It's a fun, interactive way to enjoy a game, making dining an integral part of the spectator experience.

The Bravery of the Beer Cup Snake: A phenomenon that has taken the baseball world by storm, the "beer cup snake" is as much about fan participation as it is about recycling. The concept is simple yet fascinating: fans stack their empty beer cups into a long, winding snake that slithers its way through the stands. The record-breaking instance of this was at Wrigley Field, where Chicago Cubs fans constructed a snake that was over 100 feet long, symbolizing a communal effort of epic proportions, turning waste into a work of art.

The Sweet Swing of the Churro Dog: Leave it to the Arizona Diamondbacks to revolutionize the dessert game at baseball parks. The Churro Dog, introduced in 2015, is a culinary home run featuring a warm churro nestled in a Long John chocolate-glazed donut, topped with frozen yogurt, caramel, and chocolate sauces. This decadent concoction quickly became a fan favorite, blending the comfort of classic American desserts with a twist of ballpark whimsy.

Sushi and the Seventh Inning Stretch: In the early 2000s, the Seattle Mariners introduced sushi at Safeco Field (now T-Mobile Park), breaking away from traditional ballpark fare. This marked a significant shift in baseball cuisine, catering to a diverse palate and offering fans a healthier, gourmet option. The introduction of sushi, including the now-famous "Ichiroll," named after Ichiro Suzuki, showcased the evolving tastes of baseball fans and the sport's embrace of global culinary trends.

The Dizzying Heights of the D-Bat Dog: The Arizona Diamondbacks didn't stop with the Churro Dog; they also introduced the D-Bat Dog, an 18-inch corn dog stuffed with cheddar cheese, jalapeños, and bacon, served with a side of fries. This towering treat, priced at $25, is a testament to the boldness of baseball's culinary ambitions, offering fans an over-the-top dining experience that's as memorable as the game itself.

Garlic Fries and Foggy Nights: A signature snack at Oracle Park, garlic fries have become synonymous with San Francisco Giants games. The strong aroma of garlic, paired with the crispness of the fries, creates a sensory experience that's as integral to a Giants game as the seventh-inning stretch. Originating in the late '90s, this dish has inspired other stadiums to offer their own versions, but none can quite capture the magic of the original, fog-enveloped indulgence.

The Vegetarian Victory: In a nod to changing dietary preferences, baseball stadiums across America have begun to offer a wide array of vegetarian and vegan options, from veggie dogs and burgers to plant-based nachos. This shift recognizes the growing segment of fans who seek meat-free alternatives, ensuring that the culinary experience at baseball games is inclusive, diverse, and reflective of modern eating habits. It's a win for vegetarians and the sport itself, as it adapts to the evolving tastes of its audience, proving that baseball's culinary culture is as dynamic as the game on the field.

Foul Ball Follies

Catching a Foul Ball Odds: When you're sitting in the stands at a baseball game, the odds of snagging a foul ball are roughly 1 in 835. These odds improve dramatically if you position yourself in prime locations, such as the sections extending just past the dugouts. These areas are hot spots because they're directly on the flight path of many foul balls that are hit during the game. It turns the experience into a thrilling game of chance, where your seating strategy can pay off with a memorable souvenir.

Youngest Fans' Catch: Imagine a toddler, hardly older than a baby, catching a foul ball. While there's no official record, stories circulate about children as young as three years old grabbing a foul ball with some assistance from their parents. These moments are rare and special, capturing the hearts of everyone in the stadium and those who hear about it later. It's a testament to the family-friendly nature of baseball, where even the youngest fans can become part of the game's magic.

Single-Game Foul Ball Catch Record: The record for the most foul balls caught by a fan in a single game is an impressive four. This feat was achieved by Greg Van Niel, a Cleveland Indians fan, during a game at Progressive Field. Van Niel's success required a mix of luck, skill, and strategy, including choosing the right seat and being ready at all moments. This record highlights the unique interaction between the game and its spectators, where fans can actively participate in the game, making each catch a story

Foul Ball Speeds and Safety: A foul ball can fly into the stands at speeds exceeding 100 mph. At this speed, they're faster than a speeding car on a highway and can pose a real safety risk. This is why you'll often see fans with gloves, ready to catch or deflect these high-speed surprises. It's a thrilling part of the game that requires awareness and quick reflexes, adding an element of danger to the excitement of possibly catching a ball.

Player-to-Fan Souvenirs: Beyond just foul balls, players often toss used balls into the stands as souvenirs for fans. This gesture creates a personal connection between players and fans, turning a simple baseball into a cherished keepsake. Catching a ball directly from a player can feel like a personal acknowledgment, making it an unforgettable moment for any fan.

Impactful Foul Balls: Sometimes, a fan catching a foul ball can have unintended consequences on the game. There are instances where such catches have affected the outcome of a play or even a game, inserting the fan directly into the narrative of professional baseball in unforgettable ways. These rare moments highlight the interactive and unpredictable nature of watching live sports.

Foul Balls' Wild Destinations: Not all foul balls end up in fans' hands; some find their way into peculiar spots around or outside the stadium. From becoming lodged in the stadium's architecture to floating down a nearby river, these balls embark on their own adventures. Each odd landing spot tells a story, adding to the lore and appeal of attending in-person games.

The Strategy of Catching: For some fans, catching foul balls is an art that involves careful planning, from selecting the right seat based on statistical data to predicting the play style of the batters. This strategic approach transforms the act of catching a foul ball from mere chance to a calculated endeavor, blending fandom with the thrill of the chase.

The Memory Maker: Every foul ball caught by a fan is not just a piece of sports equipment; it's a tangible memory of a unique moment shared among thousands. These balls carry stories of excitement, anticipation, and sometimes sheer luck, making them priceless to those who catch them. They serve as a physical reminder of a day at the ballpark, filled with cheers, gasps, and the joy of the game.

Architectural Wonders

Century-Old Classic: Fenway Park, nestled in the heart of Boston, Massachusetts, isn't any ballpark. Opened in 1912, it is the oldest major league ballpark still in active use. Walking into Fenway is like stepping back in time, where legends like Babe Ruth once played. Its iconic "Green Monster" left-field wall makes it a unique relic of baseball history.

Gardens in the Game: Coors Field in Denver takes "green" to a new level with its "Garden on the Grow" project. Beyond a field, it boasts a sustainable garden within its premises, producing fresh vegetables and flowers. This initiative beautifies the ballpark and educates fans on sustainability practices. It's a home run for both baseball and nature lovers!

Underwater Viewing: The Miami Marlins' stadium, Marlins Park, features a mesmerizing 30,000-gallon saltwater aquarium behind home plate. Fans can watch tropical fish dart around as players hit home runs, blending the thrill of the game with the tranquility of an underwater world. This innovative feature highlights the Marlins' commitment to combining sports with spectacular sights.

Historic Homer: On May 1, 1920, the longest Major League Baseball game in history was played between the Boston Braves and the Brooklyn Robins. The game lasted an astonishing 26 innings and was called due to darkness, ending in a 1-1 tie. This epic matchup is a testament to the endurance and passion that define baseball.

Wrigley Field's Ivy: Chicago's Wrigley Field is famous for its ivy-covered outfield walls, a unique feature that adds a touch of charm and history to the game. Planted in 1937, the ivy has become as much a part of the stadium's identity as the Cubs themselves. Balls lost in the ivy can turn singles into doubles and add an unpredictable element to the game.

PNC Park's Scenic Views: In Pittsburgh, PNC Park offers one of the most breathtaking views in sports, with its outfield opening onto the Allegheny River and a panorama of the city skyline. The Roberto Clemente Bridge and the river provide a picturesque backdrop, making every game a scenic experience.

AT&T Park's McCovey Cove: San Francisco's AT&T Park (now Oracle Park) is renowned for "McCovey Cove," the body of water beyond the right-field wall where fans in kayaks wait for home run balls to splash down. This unique feature celebrates the legendary Giants first baseman Willie McCovey and offers a distinctively San Franciscan twist to the game.

Rooftop Viewing: Wrigley Field's surrounding neighborhood, Wrigleyville, features rooftop bleachers built atop apartment buildings. These unofficial seats offer a unique vantage point to watch the games, blurring the lines between the stadium and the community and showcasing the deep bond between the Cubs and their fans.

Target Field's Self-Sustaining Water: Minneapolis's Target Field is a leader in sustainability, with a rainwater recycling system that captures, purifies, and reuses rainwater. This innovative system reduces the ballpark's water use for irrigation and cleaning, setting a new standard for environmental responsibility in sports arenas.

Yankee Stadium's Monument Park: The new Yankee Stadium preserves a slice of history with Monument Park, an open-air museum within the stadium that honors the legendary figures in Yankees history. With plaques and retired numbers, it's a sacred space where fans can connect with the heroes of the past.

Kings of the Swing

Babe Ruth's Called Shot (1932 World Series): Babe Ruth, the legendary Bambino, stepped up to the plate, the crowd's roar filling Wrigley Field. Then, he points to the center field in a move straight out of a superhero movie. Next pitch? Bam! He blasts a home run exactly where he pointed. This wasn't just a home run but a magic trick, Babe Ruth style, turning skeptics into believers one swing at a time.

Hank Aaron's 715th Home Run (1974): What about breaking a record held by Babe Ruth himself? Hank Aaron did just that on April 8, 1974, hitting his 715th home run and claiming the title for the most career home runs, a record that stood as a testament to his relentless pursuit of greatness, breaking barriers and setting new benchmarks for future generations.

Barry Bonds' Record-Setting 756th Home Run (2007): Flash forward to August 7, 2007, when Barry Bonds smashes his 756th home run, shattering Hank Aaron's record. This moment was about the distance the ball flew and also the journey Bonds took to get there, amid controversies and debates, yet undeniably etching his name in the history books.

Mark McGwire Breaking the Single-Season Record (1998): The summer of '98 was electric, with Mark McGwire and Sammy Sosa locked in a home run derby for the ages. McGwire ultimately won this duel, hitting 70 home runs and setting a new single-season record. It's a story of raw power, intense rivalry, and the chase that rekindled America's love affair with baseball.

Fernando Tatis Sr.'s Two Grand Slams in One Inning (1999): This is a mind-bender – Fernando Tatis Sr. hits not one but two grand slams in the same inning on April 23, 1999. Doing it once is tough; doing it twice is next-level. It's a record so bizarre and so unlikely that it feels more like a video game glitch than a real-life achievement.

Giancarlo Stanton's 504-Foot Monster (2016): On August 6, 2016, Giancarlo Stanton sends a baseball on a 504-foot journey, one of the longest home runs in the Statcast era. It's like hitting a ball almost one and a half football fields in length. Imagine the sheer force and precision required to send a baseball that far.

Roger Maris Breaks the Babe's Record (1961): In the year 1961, a chase that captivated a nation. Roger Maris hits 61 home runs, breaking Babe Ruth's single-season record. Amid controversy over the length of the season, Maris's achievement stands as a testament to endurance, skill, and the ability to shine under intense scrutiny and pressure.

Sammy Sosa's Three 60-Home Run Seasons (1998-2001): Sammy Sosa achieved what no other player has – three seasons with 60 or more home runs. It's a feat that speaks to consistency, power, and being a perpetual threat every time he stepped up to the plate.

Mike Trout's Rookie Record (2012): Mike Trout bursts onto the scene in 2012 with great power, hitting 30 home runs in his rookie year and setting a new standard for what it means to be a "rookie sensation" in baseball.

The Longest Home Run Ever by Mickey Mantle (1953): Legend has it, Mickey Mantle hit a home run estimated at over 600 feet in Washington's Griffith Stadium in 1953. While debates about the exact distance continue, the myth of Mantle's mammoth homer lives on, a tale of what happens when raw talent meets perfect timing.

Unbelievable Plays and Players

Rickey Henderson: The Man of Steal - Rickey Henderson is a name that reverberates through the halls of baseball history for his charismatic personality and a record so astounding, it seems unbeatable. Henderson stole 1,406 bases over his career. To put that in perspective, if you were to lay each stolen base end to end, they'd stretch over 4 miles! That's longer than crossing the Golden Gate Bridge. Henderson was really fast; he was lightning in cleats, a nightmare for pitchers and catchers alike.

Ozzie Smith: The Wizard of Oz—He was a defender so agile and fluid in his movements that he earned the nickname "The Wizard." With his acrobatic defense, Ozzie Smith turned shortstop into an art form. He made 8,375 assists in his career, a testament to his incredible skill and range. Watching Smith in the field was like witnessing a ballet, with each leap and dive more graceful than the last.

Brooks Robinson: The Human Vacuum Cleaner - Dive into the archives, and you'll find Brooks Robinson, a player who could snatch up any ball within his realm—and even some that seemed well beyond. Robinson's prowess at third base earned him 16 consecutive Gold Glove awards. His performance in the 1970 World Series was so legendary, with unbelievable plays, that fans and players alike dubbed him "The Human Vacuum Cleaner." It was as if the baseball had a magnetic attraction to his glove.

Andrelton Simmons: The Modern-Day Maestro - Fast forward to the present, and you'll meet Andrelton Simmons, a shortstop whose defensive highlights are regularly featured in sports news. Simmons has a career Defensive Runs Saved (DRS) of over 200, a metric that quantifies a player's defensive value. His ability to make plays from seemingly impossible positions has redefined what we consider within the realm of possibility for a shortstop.

Roberto Clemente: The Arm of Right Field—Transport yourself to the right field of old Forbes Field, where Roberto Clemente patrolled with an arm so powerful and accurate that base runners dared not challenge it. Clemente amassed 266 assists from right field, a testament to his extraordinary ability to throw out runners trying to advance. His arm was a weapon that kept the opposition in check.

Billy Hamilton: Speed Demon - Billy Hamilton, a modern speedster, has stolen bases at a rate that reminds us of old legends. With over 300 stolen bases in his first six seasons, Hamilton's speed is a game-changer. His lightning-fast sprints make stealing bases look as effortless as a breeze sweeping through the outfield, adding a thrilling dimension to the game that keeps fans on the edge of their seats.

Ivan Rodriguez: "Pudge" Behind the Plate - Step behind the plate with Ivan "Pudge" Rodriguez, whose arm strength and accuracy were the stuff of legends. Rodriguez threw out an astounding 46% of base stealers attempting to swipe a bag on his watch. His quick release and pinpoint accuracy made stealing second base against him seem more like a fool's errand than a strategic move.

Mark Buehrle: The No-Look Toss - Relive the moment when Mark Buehrle, a pitcher known for his quick thinking and reflexes, made a play so slick it seemed to defy physics. In a game against the Cleveland Indians, Buehrle snagged a ground ball that had ricocheted off his leg and, without looking, flipped it between his legs to first base for the out. It was a play that combined luck, skill, and a spark of boldness.

Jim Edmonds: The Man Who Flew - Cast your eyes to the outfield, where Jim Edmonds roamed, making catches that seemed to defy gravity. Edmonds made a career by turning what looked like sure hits into outs with dives and leaps that earned him eight Gold Gloves. His 1997 catch, in which he sprinted to the wall and made an over-the-shoulder catch while diving, remains one of the greatest plays in baseball history.

Javier Baez: El Mago's Tags - Lastly, witness the magic of Javier Baez, known as "El Mago" for his magical tags. Baez has a unique talent for applying tags in ways that turn stolen base attempts into an art form. His lightning-quick hands and inventive tagging techniques have made him a favorite for highlight reels and a nightmare for base stealers.

Odd and Unforgettable Moments

The Pine Tar Game (1983): In a twist straight out of a sports drama, George Brett of the Kansas City Royals launched a game-changing homer off the Yankees, only to be stopped by an umpire's ruling on the excess pine tar on his bat—a sticky situation indeed! The decision was so contentious it got reversed on appeal, and the game resumed much later, preserving Brett's blast in baseball lore.

Dock Ellis' Psychedelic No-No (1970): Dock Ellis of the Pittsburgh Pirates spun a no-hitter that became legendary, for both the rarity of the feat and because he claimed it was under the psychedelic influence of LSD. Navigating the game in such an altered state, Ellis's performance is one of baseball's most mind-bending tales.

The Great Escape Ball (1982): During a Mets-Cubs showdown, Joel Youngblood hit a ball that disappeared into a mysterious outfield drainage hole. This disappearing act led to an oddball infield double, causing both confusion and amusement.

Randy Johnson's Feathered Fastball (2001): In a freak accident that feels scripted for Hollywood, a fastball from ace Randy Johnson met an ill-fated bird mid-flight, resulting in an explosion of feathers, with the pitch ruled null. This bizarre bird strike is a stark reminder of the unpredictable nature of live sports.

Willie Mays' Miracle Catch (1954 World Series): Willie Mays, with his back to home plate, sprinted to make an iconic over-the-shoulder catch deep in center field of the Polo Grounds. This miraculous play robbed Vic Wertz and remains etched in history as perhaps the greatest defensive play ever.

10-Cent Beer Night Riot (1974): A Cleveland Indians game turned into a rowdy circus when a promotion offering 10-cent beers spiraled out of control. Drunken mayhem ensued, culminating in a forfeit to the Rangers—a sobering lesson in the dangers of excess.

The Curse of the Bambino (1918–2004): After the Boston Red Sox sold star player Babe Ruth to the New York Yankees in 1919, a superstition known as "The Curse of the Bambino" arose, claiming the Red Sox were cursed to never win another championship. This belief persisted as the team went 86 years without a World Series title, finally ending the so-called curse with their victory in 2004.

Rain Delay Rodeo: The Tarp Slide (1993): During a soggy delay, Brewers' pitcher Bob Wickman and his mates turned the infield tarp into their playground, sliding across it in a display that entertained fans and made a splash in the media.

Fernando Tatis' Grand Slam Double Feature (1999): In one inning, against the same pitcher, St. Louis Cardinal Fernando Tatis did the unthinkable—smashing two grand slams. This record-setting performance remains unmatched in Major League Baseball history.

The Steve Bartman Catastrophe (2003): A playoff game turned infamous when fan Steve Bartman deflected a critical foul ball, which potentially cost the Cubs a crucial out. The incident spiraled into a nightmarish inning, perpetuating the Cubs' "cursed" lore until their eventual 2016 triumph.

Satchel Paige's Belated Debut (1948): At 42, Satchel Paige brought his legendary pitching from the Negro Leagues to Major League Baseball, debuting with the Cleveland Indians and proving age is but a number by contributing to their World Series win.

The Imperfect Game (2010): Armando Galarraga of the Detroit Tigers was one out of a perfect game when an erroneous umpire's call at first base shattered his dream. The umpire's heartfelt apology and display of sportsmanship afterward added a poignant chapter to this story.

Statistical Wonders

The Grand Slam of Home Runs: Hitting a home run is cool, but slamming four in one game? Only 18 players in MLB's long history have managed this insane feat, with Bobby Lowe in 1894 being the first. To understand how rare this is, consider there have been over 218,400 MLB games. It's like finding a diamond in a sandbox.

Double No-Hitter Magic: Think of a pitcher who throws a no-hitter, where not a single batter from the opposing team gets a hit during the game. Now, imagine doing that twice in one season. Sounds like a fantasy, right? Johnny Vander Meer didn't think so in 1938, making him a legend for accomplishing exactly that.

The Immaculate Inning: Striking out three batters on nine consecutive pitches in a single inning is as perfect as pitching gets, hence the name "Immaculate Inning." Since 1889, this has been achieved only 105 times. Sandy Koufax, a name synonymous with pitching greatness, did this three times himself, setting a standard that's hard to beat.

Mr. 4,256: Pete Rose, a name that stirs up many feelings in the baseball world, holds the record for the most career hits at an astonishing 4,256. To put this in context, a player would need to average 200 hits for over 21 seasons even to come close. Pete Rose's record is borderline mythical.

The Iron Horse's Streak: Lou Gehrig, aka "The Iron Horse," played in 2,130 consecutive games from 1925 to 1939. This streak of durability and tenacity stood as a record for 56 years, underscoring Gehrig's almost superhuman consistency in the sport.

Mr. Perfect, 27 Times Over: In MLB history, there have been 23 perfect games where a pitcher faces exactly 27 batters and retires them all without any hits, walks, or errors. Achieving this even once is a pitcher's dream, making those who have done it part of an ultra-exclusive club.

The Strikeout King: Nolan Ryan, a name that sends shivers down batters' spines, racked up an eye-watering 5,714 strikeouts over his 27-year career. That's like striking out every batter in 190 complete games, a testament to Ryan's dominance on the mound.

The Ultimate Grand Slam: Speaking of rare, the ultimate grand slam—hitting a walk-off grand slam when down by three runs in the bottom of the ninth—has only been achieved 30 times. It's the baseball equivalent of pulling a rabbit out of a hat when everyone's watching.

The Unbreakable Barrier: Rickey Henderson, the Man of Steal, swiped 1,406 bases in his career, making him the undisputed king of theft on the diamond. This record is untouchable, with the runner-up more than 400 steals behind him.

Back-to-Back-to-Back MVPs: Winning the Most Valuable Player (MVP) award in MLB is a career highlight, but winning it three times in a row? That's a legendary move. Only one player, Barry Bonds, has achieved this rare feat, winning four consecutive MVP awards from 2001 to 2004, cementing his place in the baseball pantheon. Yogi Berra and Mike Trout, while each has won multiple MVPs, did not win three consecutive MVP awards.

Impact on Society

The National Anthem's Sporting Debut: Believe it or not, "The Star-Spangled Banner" made its major league debut way before it was officially the national anthem. During the 1918 World Series, amidst World War I, the song was played during a game, sparking a wave of patriotism, with spectators standing, hats off, and hearts racing. This moment was a home run for national unity, setting a precedent for sports events nationwide and embedding the anthem into the pre-game tradition long before it was adopted officially in 1931.

Jackie Robinson's Trailblazing Triumph: When Jackie Robinson stepped onto a Major League Baseball (MLB) field in 1947, he did more than play a game. He shattered the color barrier, challenging the status quo and becoming a towering figure in the Civil Rights Movement. Robinson's courage and talent did earn him a spot in the Hall of Fame and sparked conversations in homes and communities across the country about equality, racism, and what it means to be American.

The Linguistic Legacy: Phrases like "out of the ballpark," "touch base," and "strikeout" have slid into everyday language, making baseball's mark on American English undeniable. These idioms illustrate the sport's knack for capturing life's highs and lows, turning baseball terminology into a language of resilience, ambition, and strategy that resonates beyond the diamond.

World War II and the Rise of Women's Baseball: The All-American Girls Professional Baseball League (AAGPBL) swung into action during World War II, filling the void left by male players who'd gone to fight. This was a game-changer; a societal fastball, challenging gender norms and showcasing women's athleticism at a time when opportunities were limited. The league's legacy lives on, proving that baseball—and the courage and determination of those who play it—know no gender.

Baseball During the Great Depression: During the Great Depression baseball became more than a pastime; it was a lifeline. Teams like the New York Yankees became symbols of hope and resilience, offering an escape from everyday struggles and uniting communities. Baseball's ability to bring joy and a sense of normalcy during one of America's darkest hours underscores its role as a sport and as a beacon of light and a source of collective strength.

Integration and Social Change: Baseball's integration in the mid-20th century mirrored and propelled social change in America, challenging segregation and prejudice. As African American and Latino players began making their mark, they changed the game; they also changed hearts and minds, paving the way for a more inclusive society.

Presidential Pitches: The tradition of the President throwing the first pitch on Opening Day speaks volumes about baseball's significance in American life. Starting with William Howard Taft in 1910, this ritual has underscored the sport's status as a national pastime, symbolizing a bridge between politics, the people, and the simple joy of the game.

Baseball Cards and American Childhood: For generations, baseball cards have been more than collectibles; they've been a rite of passage. Swapping cards on playgrounds and poring over stats, kids learned about strategy, negotiation, and the thrill of the chase. These small pieces of cardboard sparked big dreams and friendships, encapsulating the innocence and excitement of childhood.

The Economic Impact: From stadium construction to employment opportunities, baseball is a major economic player, contributing significantly to local and national economies. The sport supports thousands of jobs, from vendors to professional players, and fuels industries from merchandise to broadcasting, illustrating its role as a powerhouse beyond the outfield.

Inspiring Movies and Literature: Baseball has inspired a wealth of iconic films and literature, capturing the imagination and hearts of millions. From "Field of Dreams" to "The Natural," these stories transcend the sport, exploring themes of hope, perseverance, and the timeless pursuit of dreams. Through these narratives, baseball has carved its niche in American folklore, proving that its impact goes far beyond the final score.

Baseball Brain Games And Trivia!

Game 1- Getting to Know Baseball

Engaging multiple-choice and true/false questions that cover the essentials of baseball rules, history, and terminology.

Alright! Let's step up to the plate and dive into the exciting world of baseball with a series of engaging questions designed to test and expand your knowledge of this beloved sport. Whether you're a rookie or a seasoned fan, these questions will cover the essentials of baseball rules, history, and terminology. Each question will offer multiple choice options or a true/false statement. Ready? Let's play ball!

1. The Basics of Baseball

Question 1: How many players are on the field for one team during a baseball game?

A) 9

B) 10

C) 11

D) 12

Question 2: True or False: In baseball, the term "diamond" refers to the infield layout because it resembles the shape of a diamond.

A) True

B) False

Question 3: What is a "grand slam"?

A) When a player steals four bases in a row.

B) When a team wins four games in a row.

C) When a pitcher throws four strikeouts in a row.

D) When a batter hits a home run with the bases loaded.

2. Digging Deeper: Rules and Play

Question 4: How many strikes does a batter get before they're out?

A) 1

B) 2

C) 3

D) 5

Question 5: True or False: A runner can steal a base whenever they want, even when the ball is not in play.

A) True

B) False

Question 6: What does the term "bullpen" refer to?

A) Where the team's mascot stays during the game.

B) The area where pitchers warm up before they play.

C) The dugout area for players who are not currently in the game.

D) The section of the stands is reserved for the most enthusiastic fans.

3. History and Records

Question 7: Who was known as "The Sultan of Swat"?

A) Babe Ruth

B) Hank Aaron

C) Willie Mays

D) Barry Bonds

Question 8: True or False: The New York Yankees have won more World Series titles than any other team in MLB history.

A) True

B) False

Question 9: What significant event in baseball history occurred in 1947?

A) The first-night game was played.

B) The first World Series was broadcast on television.

C) Jackie Robinson broke the color barrier.

D) The designated hitter rule was introduced.

(Solution on page 112)

Game 2 - The Big League Challenge

Game Overview:

You are a rookie in the major leagues, and your performance will determine your career trajectory and your team's success. The game now introduces a broader range of outcomes based on your decisions, considering various factors like player condition, team dynamics, and opposing team strategies.

How to Play:

Each scenario provides a backstory and detailed context, giving you information on which to base your decisions.

Outcomes give immediate results and long-term effects on your career and team morale.

Scenario 1: Defensive Positioning

Background:
You face a veteran slugger famous for his postseason heroics. He tends to hit deep into right field but has recently been struggling with fast pitches inside.

Challenge:
"How do you adjust your outfield knowing these tendencies?"
A) Shift your right fielder deeper and towards the line, risking a gap in center-right.
B) Keep the standard formation to maintain balance, preventing drastic weaknesses.
C) Move your center fielder right to cover more ground, potentially weakening left-field coverage.

Consequences: The next few games will show variations in team defensive stats based on your choice, and specific feedback will be provided on how your decision influenced game outcomes.

Scenario 2: Equipment Preparation

Background:
You're in a slump, and the coach suggests checking your equipment. You suspect your bat's grip might be affecting your swing.

Challenge:
"What adjustment do you make to your bat before the next game?"
A) Apply a fresh layer of pine tar for better grip.
B) Switch to a new bat for a change in feel.
C) Keep everything as it is to maintain consistency.

Consequences: Your choice affects your hitting performance in the next series, with detailed stats provided on swings, hits, and misses. Feedback from the coach will help you understand the impact of equipment on performance.

Scenario 3: Base Running

Background:
The game is tied in the late innings, and you're on first base. The pitcher delivers slowly, but the catcher has a strong arm. The coach gives you the signal to make a decision.

Challenge:
"What's your move?"
A) Steal second, trying to take advantage of the pitcher's slow delivery.
B) Stay put, waiting for the batter to make a hit.
C) Extend your lead slightly to improve your chances of advancing on a hit.

Consequences: Each choice leads to different play outcomes, with possible effects on the next innings and commentary on how your decision played out over the game.

Scenario 4: Playoff Strategy

Background:

It's a high-stress playoff game, and your team needs a boost. You're known for both power and contact hitting.

Challenge:

"Facing a tired pitcher, what's your strategy?"

A) Go for a big hit, trying to energize the team and fans.

B) Focus on getting on base in any way possible.

C) Take pitches, aiming to draw a walk.

Consequences: The outcome of your at-bat affects not just this game but also your reputation and confidence, influencing your stats and interactions for the remainder of the playoffs.

Scenario 5: Championship Decisions

Background:

In game 7, late innings, the pressure is immense. You're pitching against the top of the opponent's lineup, and the game is tied.

Challenge:

"You have a couple of base runners and a dangerous hitter up next. Your pitch?"

A) Challenge him with your best fastball.

B) Trick him with an off-speed pitch.

C) Intentionally walk him to face a less dangerous batter.

Consequences: The decision impacts this at-bat, team morale, and personal stats as a pitcher.

(Solution on page 114)

Game 3 - Fill-in-the-Blanks

Welcome to the **Fill-in-the-Blanks: Baseball Edition**! You'll encounter sentences with missing words, all related to the world of baseball. Your mission is to fill in the blanks with the correct baseball terms. Ready to swing for the fences? Let's play ball!

Don't worry if you don't hit a home run on your first try; this game is about learning and having fun!

Round 1: The Basics

1. In baseball, the player who throws the ball towards the hitter is called the _____.

2. The area in which the game is played is known as the _____.

3. A _____ is a hit that allows the batter to reach third base safely.

4. When a batter manages to hit the ball out of the park, it's called a _____.

5. The player responsible for catching balls in the outfield is known as the _____.

Round 2: Getting Technical

1. The defensive move where the ball is quickly thrown to the base ahead of the runner to get them out is called a _____.

2. A pitch that's thrown with the intention of being difficult to hit, often resulting in a swing and a miss, is termed a _____.

3. The term for a game or part of a game where a pitcher does not allow any hits is a _____.

4. A _____ is a hit that barely goes over the infielders' heads and lands in the outfield for a hit.

5. The protective gear worn by the player catching the pitches is known as the _____.

Round 3: Legends and Lore

1. The famous player known as "The Sultan of Swat" is _____.

2. _____ Robinson broke the color barrier in Major League Baseball.

3. The infamous curse that was said to have prevented the Boston Red Sox from winning the World Series for 86 years is known as the Curse of the _____.

4. The 1927 New York Yankees, known for their powerful lineup, were dubbed the _____.

5. The record for most home runs in a single season was famously set by _____.

(Solution on page 117)

Who Am I? Baseball Legends Edition

How to Play:

Read the Clue: Start with the first clue for each personality.

Make a Guess: Think about who the clue could describe. If you're unsure, wait for more clues.

Use as Few Clues as Possible: Try to guess the personality with the fewest clues to show your baseball knowledge.

Check Your Answer: Compare your guess with the answer provided on the answers page.

Puzzle #1

Clue 1: I am known as the all-time leader in stolen bases in MLB history.

Clue 2: I played most of my career with the Oakland Athletics, becoming a symbol of speed and agility on the bases.

Clue 3: I was a prolific leadoff hitter, leading the league in walks four times and runs scored five times.

Clue 4: I was inducted into the Baseball Hall of Fame in 2009. My career spanned four decades, from the late 1970s to the early 2000s.

Answer :

Puzzle #2

Clue 1: I began my MLB career as a standout pitcher for the Boston Red Sox before becoming one of the most renowned sluggers.

Clue 2: I set a record for 60 home runs in a single season in 1927, a record that stood until 1961.

Clue 3: The infamous trade that sent me from Boston to New York is said to have cursed the Red Sox for decades.

Clue 4: Known as "The Great Bambino," my larger-than-life persona is still celebrated in baseball folklore.

Answer :

Puzzle #3

Clue 1: My dedication to humanitarian causes was as well known as my skills in the right field.

Clue 2: I was the first Caribbean-born player to be inducted into the Hall of Fame, representing Puerto Rico with pride.

Clue 3: I ended my career with exactly 3,000 hits, a milestone achieved in my final at-bat.

Answer :

Puzzle #4

Clue 1: Known for my towering height and powerful pitching, I made my MLB debut in 1988.

Clue 2: I am one of the few pitchers who have won the Cy Young Award in both the American and National Leagues.

Clue 3: My intimidating fastball helped me lead the majors in strikeouts nine times.

Clue 4: I was a key player in the Arizona Diamondbacks 2001 World Series victory.

Answer :

Puzzle #5

Clue 1: I broke Babe Ruth's record for career home runs, holding the title until it was surpassed by Barry Bonds.

Clue 2: I also hold records for the most RBIs and total bases in MLB history.

Clue 3: I faced significant racial adversity during my quest to break the home run record.

Clue 4: My career was mostly spent with the Braves, both in Milwaukee and Atlanta.

Answer :

Puzzle #6

Clue 1: My dominance on the mound was showcased during the 1960s when I became a symbol of pitching excellence.

Clue 2: During my career, I pitched four no-hitters, including a perfect game.

Clue 3: I won three Cy Young Awards, each time unanimously, a testament to my mastery during those seasons.

Clue 4: Despite my success, I retired at the age of 30 due to persistent arm injuries.

Answer :

(Solution on page 119)

Game 5 – Match the Record

Instructions:

Objective: Correctly match each baseball legend with its corresponding record or achievement.

How to Play:

1. Link each baseball legend to one of the achievements listed.

2. Record your matches on paper.

3. Review the provided solutions to evaluate your performance.

4. **Final Review:** Compare your answers with the solutions to test your knowledge of baseball history.

Baseball Legends:

- A. Joe DiMaggio

- B. Rickey Henderson

- C. Ted Williams

- D. Cal Ripken Jr.

- E. Willie Mays

- F. Nolan Ryan

- G. Barry Bonds

- H. Cy Young

- I. Roger Clemens

Records or Achievements:

1. Most Career Wins by a Pitcher (511)

2. Only Player in MLB History to Win 7 Cy Young Awards

3. Member of both the 500 Home Run and 3,000 Hit Clubs

4. Consecutive Games Played (2,632)

5. Most Career Home Runs (762)

6. Most Career No-Hitters (7)

7. Last Player to Hit Over .400 in a Season (.406 in 1941)

8. All-Time Leader in Stolen Bases (1,406)

9. 56-Game Hitting Streak

How to Match:

Assign each legend (A-I) to the record or achievement they are most famously known for from the list (1-9).

(Solution on page 120)

Game 6 – What Comes Next?

How to Play:

Read each scenario, which is drawn from real baseball situations.
Strategize and Decide: Apply your baseball knowledge to figure out the next event in the play.
Select Your Answer: Choose what you believe is the correct outcome.
Check and Learn: Compare your guess with the correct answer and read the explanation to deepen your understanding of baseball.
Batter up! Let's see if you can hit a grand slam with your knowledge this time.

Scenario 1:

A curveball is thrown, and the batter connects, sending a fly ball straight into the waiting glove of the center fielder, who catches it cleanly. What comes next?
A) The batter heads to first base.
B) The batter is ruled out.
C) A time-out is requested.
Your Answer:

Scenario 2:

With the bases loaded, the batter hits a ground ball to the shortstop, who fields it and throws it to the second baseman. The second baseman steps on second base before the runner from first can reach it. What comes next?
A) The runner from second proceeds to third base.
B) The batter is awarded first base.

C) The runner from first is out at second base.

Your Answer:

Scenario 3:

A runner on first base watches as the batter hits a high fly ball to right field. The right fielder catches it, and after the catch, the runner tags up and dashes towards second base. What comes next?

A) The runner must retreat to first base.

B) The runner attempts to reach second base safely.

C) The inning concludes.

Your Answer:

Scenario 4:

In a tie game at the bottom of the 9th inning with two outs, the batter hits a towering fly ball. It's unclear if it will land in fair territory for a home run or foul. What comes next?

A) The umpires wait for the ball to land.

B) The umpires initiate a video replay review to determine the ball's status.

C) The batter circles the bases, hoping it's a home run.

Your Answer:

(Solution on page 121)

Game 7 - Arrange the Historic Moments

Players put significant events in baseball history in chronological order based solely on text descriptions.

Dive into the heart of baseball's rich history with this interactive challenge. Your task is to place significant events in their precise chronological order, using detailed descriptions to guide you. This game is designed to test your knowledge and deepen your appreciation for baseball's pivotal moments, from its earliest innovations to its most celebrated achievements.

The Events to Arrange

1. **Hank Aaron Breaks Babe Ruth's Home Run Record**

   ○ Description: Hank Aaron hit his 715th career home run, surpassing Babe Ruth's longstanding record. This event was a significant milestone in baseball history, reflecting Aaron's resilience and excellence in the face of adversity.

2. **The Introduction of Night Games**

   ○ Description: The Cincinnati Reds hosted the Philadelphia Phillies in MLB's first official night game at Crosley Field, introducing illuminated evening play to the sport. This innovation made baseball more accessible to fans who worked during the day.

3. **Alexander Cartwright Codifies Baseball Rules**

   ○ Description: Often credited with laying down the foundational rules of modern baseball, Alexander Cartwright formalized aspects such as dia-mond-shaped infield, foul lines, and the three-strike rule. This pivotal moment marked the birth of baseball as we know it.

4. Jackie Robinson Breaks the Color Barrier

- Description: Jackie Robinson made his debut with the Brooklyn Dodgers, shattering Major League Baseball's color barrier and paving the way for racial integration in professional sports.

5. The First World Series

- Description: The inaugural World Series marks the championship contest of Major League Baseball, pitting the American League's champion against that of the National League. It symbolized the unification of the two leagues under the banner of national competition.

6. The Shot Heard 'Round the World

- Description: In a dramatic finish to the National League pennant race, Bobby Thomson hit a game-winning home run for the New York Giants against the Brooklyn Dodgers. This moment is etched in baseball lore for its dramatic impact and representation of the game's unpredictability.

Your Task

Now, with the events and their dates in hand, arrange them in chronological order from the earliest to the most recent.

(Solution on page 123)

Solutions – Baseball Brain Games And Trivia!

Game 1- Getting to Know Baseball (Solution)

1. The Basics of Baseball

Question 1: *A) 9*. Each team has nine players on the field when they are playing defense.

Question 2: *A) True*. The diamond refers to the four bases (home plate, first base, second base, and third base) laid out in a diamond shape.

Question 3: *D) When a batter hits a home run with the bases loaded*. This is the maximum number of runs (four) that can be scored on a single hit.

2. Digging Deeper: Rules and Play

Question 4: *C) 3*. A batter is allowed two strikes before the third one causes them to be out.

Question 5: *B) False*. A runner can only attempt to steal a base when the ball is in play.

Question 6: *B) The area where pitchers warm up before they play*. It's typically located just beyond the outfield.

3. History and Records

Question 7: *A) Babe Ruth*. He was one of the most famous players in baseball history and earned his nickname due to his incredible hitting power.

Question 8: *A) True*. The New York Yankees hold the record for the most World Series championships.

Question 9: *C) Jackie Robinson broke the color barrier.* He became the first African American to play in Major League Baseball in the modern era.

How did you do? Whether you hit a home run or struck out on a few, I hope this journey through the basics of baseball was both informative and enjoyable. Remember, every great player started as a rookie, so keep building your knowledge and love for the game!

(Questions on page 93)

Game 2 - The Big League Challenge (Solution)

Scenario 1:

Given typical conditions and assuming a relatively balanced team capability, **Option B** might be the most prudent choice for most situations. It provides a conservative approach that allows the pitcher to use a varied pitching strategy without overcommitting the field to specific threats. It relies on maintaining a balanced defense that is capable of adapting to different outcomes during the game.

By choosing **Option B**, the team avoids creating significant weaknesses in the field setup, providing flexibility to adapt to the game's flow and how the slugger responds in his at-bat. This decision could be particularly effective if the pitcher has a diverse arsenal and can mix pitches to keep the slugger guessing, reducing the likelihood of a big hit to a specific area.

While each option has its strategic merit, maintaining a balanced defense often offers the most stable approach, especially in a high-stakes or uncertain game scenario.

Scenario 2:

Given the scenario where a slump is in question and suspicion about the bat's grip affecting performance, **Option A (Apply a fresh layer of pine tar for better grip)** appears to be the most directly beneficial choice. It addresses the player's concern about the bat's grip and provides a practical solution that can immediately positively impact performance without major adjustments.

This choice supports a proactive approach to dealing with a slump by making a small but potentially significant change to the equipment, which can boost confidence and effectiveness at the plate.

By selecting this option, players can experience a tangible improvement in their interaction with the bat. This allows them to focus more on their swing mechanics and less on maintaining their grip, hopefully leading to a quicker end to the slump.

Scenario 3:

Given the tied game in late innings, the pressure is high, and each decision carries weight. **Option C (Extend your lead slightly to improve your chances of advancing on a hit)** seems to provide a balanced approach. It increases the likelihood of advancing on base hits while mitigating the risk of being thrown out at second as compared to a full steal. This option allows you to react quickly to hits and take advantage of any mishaps by the defense without committing fully to a high-risk steal.

This choice capitalizes on the pitcher's slow delivery by enhancing your readiness to advance without fully committing to a risky play that could end the inning prematurely. It's a strategic compromise that optimizes your position on base, keeping the inning alive and maintaining pressure on the defense.

Scenario 4:

Given that the background emphasizes a high-stress situation and a tired pitcher, **Option C (Take pitches, aiming to draw a walk)** might be the most strategically advantageous. This approach maximizes the chance of exploiting the pitcher's fatigue without risking an out from an aggressive swing. It plays a patient game, potentially leading to better pitches for following hitters or forcing a pitching change if the pitcher continues to struggle.

By drawing a walk, you're also conserving energy and focusing on mental discipline, which can be crucial in the later stages of a playoff game. This choice positions you safely on base and maintains pressure on the opposing team, increasing their stress and potentially leading to errors or strategic missteps.

Scenario 5:

Given the high stakes of a tied Game 7 in the World Series and depending on the specific details of the game situation (which aren't provided here but should be considered), **Option B (Trick him with an off-speed pitch)** might be the most strategic choice. This option allows for maintaining an aggressive approach to getting out while minimizing the risk associated with the batter's potential strength against fastballs. It leverages the element of surprise and the psychological pressure of the moment, potentially leading to a crucial out without the risk of a big hit associated with a fastball or increasing the base runners with a walk.

This decision strategically plays to the pitcher's advantage by using unpredictability and the pitcher's skill in off-speed delivery. The goal is to aim for a crucial out in a tense moment, which could decisively maintain the game's balance and momentum in your team's favor.

(Questions on page 96)

Game 3 - Fill-in-the-Blanks (Solution)

Round 1: The Basics

1. In baseball, the player who throws the ball toward the hitter is called the **pitcher**.

2. The area in which the game is played is known as the **field**.

3. A **triple** is a hit that allows the batter to reach third base safely.

4. When a batter manages to hit the ball out of the park, it's called a **home run**.

5. The player responsible for catching balls in the outfield is known as the **outfielder**.

Round 2: Getting Technical

1. The defensive move where the ball is quickly thrown to the base ahead of the runner to get them out is called a **putout or force out**.

2. A pitch that's thrown with the intention of being difficult to hit, often resulting in a swing and a miss, is termed a **strikeout pitch or breaking ball**.

3. The term for a game or part of a game where a pitcher does not allow any hits is a **no-hitter**.

4. A **Texas Leaguer** is a hit that barely goes over the infielders' heads and lands in the outfield for a hit.

5. The protective gear worn by the player catching the pitches is known as the **catcher's equipment**.

Round 3: Legends and Lore

1. The famous player known as "The Sultan of Swat" is **Babe Ruth**.

2. **Jackie Robinson** broke the color barrier in Major League Baseball.

3. The infamous curse that was said to have prevented the Boston Red Sox from winning the World Series for 86 years is known as the Curse of the **Bambino**.

4. The 1927 New York Yankees, known for their powerful lineup, were dubbed **Murderers' Row**.

5. The record for most home runs in a single season was famously set by **Barry Bonds**.

(Questions on page 99)

Game 4 – Who Am I? (Solution)

Answers to "Who Am I? Baseball Legends Edition"

Puzzle #1 **Answer:** Rickey Henderson

Puzzle #2 **Answer:** Babe Ruth

Puzzle #3 **Answer:** Roberto Clemente

Puzzle #4 **Answer:** Randy Johnson

Puzzle #5 **Answer:** Hank Aaron

Puzzle #6 **Answer:** Sandy Koufax

(Questions on page 101)

Game 5 - Match the Record (Solution)

- Most Career Wins by a Pitcher (511) - **H. Cy Young**: Cy Young's record for career wins stands strong.

- Only Player in MLB History to Win 7 Cy Young Awards - **I. Roger Clemens**: Roger Clemens won 7 Cy Young Awards.

- Member of both the 500 Home Run and 3,000 Hit Clubs - **E. Willie Mays**: Willie Mays is renowned for being a member of the elite 500 Home Run and 3,000 Hit clubs.

- Consecutive Games Played (2,632) - **D. Cal Ripken Jr**.: Cal Ripken Jr. set the record for consecutive games played.

- Most Career Home Runs (762) - **G. Barry Bonds**: Barry Bonds holds the record for the most career home runs.

- Most Career No-Hitters (7) - **F. Nolan Ryan**: Nolan Ryan is famous for throwing seven no-hitters.

- Last Player to Hit Over .400 in a Season (.406 in 1941) - **C. Ted Williams**: Ted Williams famously hit over .400 in 1941.

- All-Time Leader in Stolen Bases (1,406) - **B. Rickey Henderson**: Rickey Henderson is the all-time leader in stolen bases.

- 56-Game Hitting Streak - **A. Joe DiMaggio**: Joe DiMaggio set the record for a 56-game hitting streak.

(Questions on page 104)

Game 6 - What Comes Next? (Solution)

Scenario 1:

Correct Answer: B) The batter is ruled out. This play is an example of a "flyout," where a ball hit into the air is caught before it lands. According to the rules, the batter is out in such situations, preventing them from advancing to first base.

Scenario 2:

Correct Answer: C) The runner from first is out at second base. This is a classic "force out" situation. When the bases are loaded, the runner from first is forced to advance to second because the batter becomes a runner. The shortstop's quick action to get the ball to the second baseman, who touches the base before the runner from first arrives, results in the runner being out. This strategic play prevents the runners from advancing freely and adds a layer of tactical depth to the game.

Scenario 3:

Correct Answer: B) The runner attempts to reach second base safely. This scenario demonstrates the "tag up" rule. After a fly ball is caught, runners may advance to the next base, but only after touching the base they occupied at the time of the catch. This rule balances risk and reward, encouraging intelligent base running and strategic decisions.

Scenario 4:

Correct Answer: A) The umpires wait for the ball to land. In modern baseball, umpires must first observe where the ball lands to make an initial call on whether it is a home run or foul. If the situation is ambiguous or contested after the ball has landed, umpires or a manager may then initiate a video replay review to ensure the decision is as accurate as possible, especially in critical game moments. This adherence to procedure respects the integrity of the game and the efforts of the players.

(Questions on page 106)

Game 7 – Arrange the Historic Moments (Solution)

1. **Alexander Cartwright Codifies Baseball Rules (1845)**

   o Cartwright's contributions laid the groundwork for the standardization of baseball, facilitating its growth as a structured sport.

2. **The First World Series (1903)**

   o The initiation of the World Series established a competitive pinnacle for professional baseball, fostering a new era of sport.

3. **The Introduction of Night Games (May 24, 1935)**

   o Night games transformed the accessibility of baseball, broadening its fan base and altering how the sport was consumed and enjoyed.

4. **Jackie Robinson Breaks the Color Barrier (April 15, 1947)**

   o Robinson's debut was a significant event in the American civil rights movement, heralding a new era of societal progress.

5. **The Shot Heard 'Round the World (October 3, 1951)**

   o This thrilling moment captured the essence of baseball's unpredictability and drama, becoming a symbol of the sport's capacity to unite and captivate.

6. **Hank Aaron Breaks Babe Ruth's Home Run Record (April 8, 1974)**

   o This underlined his perseverance and excellence, breaking a record that had stood for decades and making a profound statement against racism.
   (Questions on page 108)

Afterword

Wow, you've made it to the end of our baseball journey! Thanks for hanging out with me through these stories and fun facts. Whether you were blown away by Babe Ruth, inspired by Jackie Robinson, or laughed at wild fan moments, I hope something here stuck with you.

Hey, one last thing before you go, if you enjoyed this journey, drop a review – it really makes my day to hear from you. I read every single review, and it helps get these stories out to more people. Let me know for example which chapter you liked the most or what kind of book you'd like me to write next. Just scan the QR code to leave your review ;)

Want to see more books I made for you? Same, just scan the QR code below and check it out; there is always something amazing there you would love to read!

Thanks Y'all ! ... Harris

Made in United States
Orlando, FL
29 September 2024

51872106R00075